To Bianna
with Love, Peace, Joy
comfort and many
Miracles !

D1521140

Never Alone

Carmenta Jean Baptiste

Never Alone
The Orphan Who Hid Thousands of Feelings Behind

Copyright © 2023 by Carmenta Jean Baptiste

ISBN: 979-8-8507-6907-9

Printed in the United States of America

For permissions, inquiries, or other requests, please contact:
carmentajeanbaptiste@gmail.com.

DEDICATION

This book is dedicated to those who feel empty inside and believe that no one is there for them. Know that God has already set you free and He is there for you, no matter what you're going through. I love all of you, and I've been where you are right now.

I also dedicate this book to everyone around me who gave me the strength to keep going, even when I felt like giving up.

CONTENTS

ACKNOWLEDGMENTS

To my mom, April Kayatin: You never gave up on me, even when life was incredibly hard. I pray that God always provides for you and blesses your life in unimaginable ways. You have shown me what real love is, never giving up on me. The promises you made years ago, you kept them alive, and that is the epitome of real love. It doesn't mean we didn't face difficult times, but you remained true to your promises. You are my hero, and may God continue to bless your soul. Know that you have a special place deep inside my heart. I love you so much.

To my Dad's cousin who I like to call grandma, Madan Rosalvot: You believed in me and knew I could be anything. Although you passed away right before my life changed, your love continues to soar high. I will love you forever.

To the Kayatin family, who always makes me feel like I have a place no matter what.

To all who love Haiti, you are a part of my success.

To everyone who sent me letters before I came to the United States, may the Lord bless you abundantly beyond your imagination. May His blessings be your resource when your cup runs dry.

INTRODUCTION

Knowing who I am in Christ has been the most powerful revelation in my life. Knowing that I am loved by the Creator has been my sunlight and realizing that I can do all things through Him has been my strength to keep living. I spent my entire life searching for love, and when I found it, I never regretted it. I want to thank God for teaching me how to love others as He has loved me. He is the reason I am still alive and the reason I never gave up a long time ago. He is also the reason I stood up in the face of difficulties. Be confident in who you are in Christ and never doubt Him. Always remember that you are loved by the greatest God of all. Knowing that you can do everything through Him is an extra source of strength, making you more secure in yourself.

If you ever feel like giving up, this book is for you. My journey of success is not for me alone, which is why I am sharing my story with you. You are worth more than what you're going through, and you are stronger than the problems that try to keep you down. You have the power to fight because you are amazing. May this book bless you as you read it. May it help you understand that life is a series of trials we all go through, but that giving up is never an option. You will find comfort within these pages. As long as I have breath in my body, I will do my best to encourage you. Here are two of my favorite verses that have helped me:

Philippians 4:13 - *"I can do all things through Christ who strengthens me."* (NIV)

1 Corinthians 13:13 - *"And now these three remain: faith, hope and love but the greatest of these is love."* (NIV)

As we navigate life, we go through ups and downs as a natural part of our human experience. From situations to relationships to business opportunities, we go through various things that cause us to go from happy to sad, angry to disappointed, and all of these things are necessary for our personal growth. I chose to write this book because I realized that my life story fully shows that God can turn a mess into a message. As I have learned to walk in faith, I've come to acknowledge that God has turned my pain into happiness. He has given me beauty for ashes.

I grew up in an orphanage, which led me to deal with identity issues. Not knowing my family or how my mother and father looked caused my childhood to be miserable. Seeing other children visiting with their families made me sad to the point that I questioned whether I had any family. The feelings of loneliness were so intense I started to experience negative self-talk as a result. I would tell myself that I am useless or that I'm not worth it. It felt like there were people in the orphanage who reinforced these negative statements through their interactions with me.

I knew enough to lean on God in those low moments. Although I had no knowledge of my earthly family, I came to embrace that God is able to do exceedingly and abundantly above the things I can ask or think. My desire to know my family was valid, and there was nothing inherently wrong with that, but I came to see how faithful God has been to me, and ultimately He gave me a family.

The journey to finding a family was extremely challenging. There were many times I wanted to give up. As a matter of fact, there were times that I lost all hope. I remember being hyper focused on the low moments and struggling to tap into my strength. It became easy to feel like life was over, but that belief was always short lived. The beauty of this experience is that in regaining my strength and learning not to give up, I recognized that the journey forward would allow me to experience a testimony that I'm able to share with you in this book. Everything that happened, happened for a reason.

In this book, my goal is to share with you how to overcome adversity. You will learn how to be intentional about understanding who you are as an individual so that as you are navigating life, you're able to be resilient and come out on top. Once you learn the formula that applies to your journey, intentional execution will guarantee your success.

I also want to ensure that your takeaways include understanding that you should never give up on yourself. Things in life have a way of turning upside down but understand that you have the power to correct your course or change directions altogether. Learning to pivot will serve you well.

Beyond this, there will be many things that come to distract you, but again, you have the power to shift your focus. You may have many different reasons to give up, but when it comes to the things you were purposed to do, you must pursue those things with everything in you.

As you navigate this book, I believe you would benefit from allowing yourself to translate my experiences into questions you can ask yourself as you navigate your own journey. At the end of each chapter is a section of reflection questions that will allow you to explore your own journey. Some of these questions may incite you to consider triggers and trauma that need to be uprooted. Do not be afraid of this process. While it is not easy to dig up the roots of negativity in your life, it is a necessary process to facilitate your personal growth.

In addition to the reflection questions, if you have the accompanying guided journal, you will be able to delve into things that help you to build your faith as you are rebuilding you! With encouraging scriptures, short prayers, meditation questions and journal prompts, these are tools that will allow you to work through some of the things that have affected your ability to navigate life effectively.

Thank you for your willingness to journey with me through my story, and for your willingness to invest in yourself. Cheers to the journey!

CHAPTER 1:

LEARNING MY IDENTITY

I grew up in an orphanage, not knowing any of my family. Unfortunately, both of my parents had passed away. At the orphanage, I found myself as the first girl and the thirteenth child to be placed there. Let me delve a little deeper and share some of the blessings I experienced along the way.

Living in an orphanage was far from easy, especially when my thoughts and opinions clashed with those in authority over me. It felt disheartening to be constantly at odds with their expectations, as if living in an orphanage was the last thing I could ever desire. School was a particularly challenging environment, as I would hear people say, "The orphanage kids are here," and that was hurtful. While we may have garnered attention initially, the label of being orphans quickly overshadowed any popularity we may have had. Each of us was assigned a number to identify our clothes, and upon arriving at school, people would refer to us by those numbers.

It was a constant reminder of our circumstances, and we endured the pain until the day they stopped labeling us in such a way.

However, the impact of being an orphan lingered for a long time. Every time someone mentioned it, tears would well up in my eyes. It was a painful reality, especially because I was a true orphan among the children there. Some of my peers had one parent, and others had both, which allowed them to say, "I have parents." I couldn't claim the same because I didn't have either. In those moments, I clung to my faith and my inner strength. I tried my hardest not to let the emotions overwhelm me, but whenever a parent arrived to pick up their child, I couldn't help but feel sadness, wondering when my own parents would come and greet me with affectionate words. Sadly, that day never came.

The pain continued to accumulate, and tears became familiar for me. It became a part of who I was. In Haiti, where I grew up, being an orphan meant being seen as someone without dreams, without a vision, without a future, and without any talents. I internalized their perception and began to believe that I was truly nothing, solely because of my orphan status. It became my deepest scar, my biggest weakness, and my greatest fear in life. I was so scared that I would never be anything in life. All I could think of was how my life in the future would be nothing because I was an orphan.

Sometimes I would pray and honestly question God, asking if I was a mistake, but He didn't answer me. Little did I know that He was preparing something beyond the capacity of my mind to comprehend or accept. It was later in life that I understood His purpose and realized that He had given me the strength and the words necessary to reach the goals for the purpose He had set for me. And now, reflecting on your own life's phase, I encourage you to do the same—to hold onto your faith, find strength within, and keep pursuing the path that He has set before you.

One thing for sure: I never gave up on my prayers. Sometimes, all you can do is pray and let God take care of the rest. No matter what you're going through, there will always be a breakthrough. Your brokenness means nothing to God Almighty. He has the power to use your broken pieces and put you back together, piece by piece.

When people hear or see my life story, it may seem like the worst thing that could happen to a child. But let me tell you, don't worry about those things. They won't last forever. Nothing is impossible for God. Even when you feel like life is over, it's not. In fact, it's just the beginning. God is always there for you, just one step away. Don't hesitate to cry out to Him when you feel like you can't go on. He will always be there for you.

I know there are times when we become impatient waiting for God to move those mountains. But have faith because those mountains are about to move for you. It is your faith that will lead you to where you need to be.

Without faith, you won't be able to move towards your dreams. You'll feel stuck, and that's not a pleasant feeling when you know what's holding you back. Just let God write His story with you as the main character. I let Him use me as an empty page, and you are now a witness to the book He has written. You're not just an empty page; you become the living testimony of His grace. And all it takes is a little faith to step out of your comfort zone.

You don't have to accomplish everything alone. Trust in the Holy Spirit and you will have help. Life has taught me that God always finds a way, even if you blew the first opportunity. There's no need to feel ashamed because we have all been there. It's not easy to just let something or someone control our lives. That "someone" is a miracle-working God who continues to be present in my life stories. This is not the end, but rather the beginning of what He is about to do.

I believe it, and now it's your turn to believe that He can elevate you to a different level. At that level, you won't even be able to comprehend the greatness that awaits you. All you have to do is walk by faith, even when it feels like you're walking blindly. Let God lead you to wherever He needs you to be. Trust in Him to lead you as you embrace the journey ahead.

A Child of God

I think it's awesome to be called a child of God. To think that I am recognized as a child by the mighty God, who is not moved by anything on this earth, fills me with a profound sense of wonder. But I must admit that I haven't always been obedient to my Heavenly Father. There have been moments when I've chosen to disobey, but the beautiful truth is that He always forgives me for my mistakes. He extends His forgiveness to all His children.

Children often make foolish choices and act in foolish ways, but our earthly parents still choose to forgive us. In the same way, our Heavenly Father forgives us when we stumble and make wrong decisions. Being a child of God is a remarkable and beautiful thing, but the truth is that it can also be challenging at times because it requires us to endure suffering and pain.

Growing up without an earthly father was incredibly painful for me. I often found myself thinking about it, especially on Father's Day. I would see other children celebrating their dads while I stood alone, feeling a deep sense of sadness and longing. I came to realize that I have a Heavenly Father who claims me as His own, which made me grateful and proud, but it still made me sad that I didn't have a dad with whom I could have a human experience.

As time passed, I came to understand that not physically seeing or touching God doesn't diminish His presence in my life. He touches me deeply when I feel like giving up on everything I'm going through. Now, I feel secure in the knowledge that I have Him as my primary source of support and guidance. To be called a child of God carries a lot of strength and comfort. I never thought I would feel so secure in being recognized as His child. Even as an adult, I am still proud of being called a child of His. The love that comes with this identity has been my source of strength, propelling me forward.

If you've lost one or both of your parents, know that God wants you to call Him Father and desires to embrace you as His child. He will care for you, allowing you to stand tall and take pride in the person you are becoming. Sometimes it feels like life gave me a reason to stop living and just complain about not having parents, but God has shown me that He is enough. He is willing to walk with you through every moment of your life, claiming you as His own.

With each passing day, my love for God grows, and I become more and more proud of the incredible things He has accomplished in my life and continues to do. Accepting a Father whom I cannot physically touch or cry on has not been an easy journey. There have been moments when I've been in pain, and in those moments, I call out to Him, questioning why certain things were allowed to happen. In those moments, I feel His presence right where I am. I take a deep breath, acknowledging that He is here with me, and that I am not forgotten and never will be.

If you feel the need for a father's presence, or if you find yourself without one, turn to Him. He provides real comfort and fills the void within me. And rest assured, He will do the same for you.

In learning to see myself as a daughter of the most high God, I have learned to stand firm in my identity. Nothing in this world can move me. I want to encourage you to ask yourself, "Do I know who I am?" Understand that you are a child of God, no different than I am. You are not defined by your scars, your pain, your problems, your self-doubt, or your past. You are not useless. You are chosen by God, a beacon of light for others, a source of living water for those who thirst. You are uniquely you, God's beloved and a manifestation of His grace. Believe it, even if it's hard at times, because that is the truth of who you are.

You cannot change your inherent identity. Discovering my true identity has been a journey, one filled with fear and doubt. Sometimes I have questioned if I truly deserve the blessings in my life, feeling as if I don't deserve them because of past mistakes. However, I refuse to let those doubts overshadow my understanding of who I truly am in God.

So, remember, you are a child of the most high God, deeply loved by Him. Don't let your past actions diminish your sense of self-worth and purpose. The mistakes you made in the past hold no power over your present and future unless you give them that power. It is natural to sometimes be afraid of embracing the fullness of your identity, but they should not control the talents and potential that reside within you.

Today, I want you to confidently declare that you are more than enough. If God has declared His sufficiency for me, then He does the same for you. Just be intentional in listening and responding when His voice calls out to you. His voice reveals the truth of who you are, and only God truly knows the depths of your identity.

The Struggle Is Real
We often find ourselves struggling and wondering why. We

struggle because it is an inevitable part of our journey, something we must navigate through. We cry over painful experiences and the aspects of life that we cannot comprehend. We cry because we cannot understand how our path has unfolded, and we cry because we feel powerless to change our situation. Acknowledge that the struggle is real, and while we may not have control over its presence, we can fight to overcome it.

It felt like at one point that the struggle became a part of who I am. I remember I would wake up crying, asking God, "Why??" I would ask why I had no family and why I had to be sent to the orphanage. I felt like I had no sense of identity and wondered if I would ever catch a break.

As time went on, I began to understand that God was showing me how to endure, how to resist and rise above my struggles. I realized that struggles would always be a part of my life. I had to learn how to fight and overcome them. To those who are currently struggling and feel trapped, the solution is simpler than you might think: Believe in yourself and learn how to handle your struggles, much like tackling everyday chores.

Life is far from easy, and struggles come bundled with all the drama we face in life. But understanding that you have power over your struggles is amazing. You can confront them, but only if you have faith in yourself. If you lack belief in your abilities, struggles will persist and continue to overwhelm you. Struggles are there to give you strength, to teach you how to fight your battles. If you fail to resist struggles, you won't elevate to a higher level.

Know your true identity, stand up for yourself, and elevate yourself to new heights. Struggles can sometimes be so overpowering that they make you question yourself. I allowed my struggles to overshadow my true self, and it pained me to know that they had this control over me. Growing up in Haiti, I witnessed people enduring hardships just to get bread to eat. I believed that our struggles were unique and that we alone understood their true meaning.

Later, when I came to the United States, I discovered a different kind of struggle, one that felt even more real. It involved the constant pursuit of desires, needs, and obligations. It manifested as anxiety, stress, and an unrelenting burden. The struggle I faced here was different from what I experienced back home. It realized the struggle in the States is rooted in selfishness and the desire to possess what others have. It is undeniably real, and learning to live with that was hard.

However, I have come to accept it, realizing that it is not our fault. It is what the world has taught us. But we must also recognize that there comes a point where we aren't controlling the struggles and they begin to control us because we surrender too much power to them.

CHAPTER 2:

PRAYER & FORGIVENESS:
A JOURNEY OF THE HEART

I always said that if I couldn't take care of my own child, I would never subject them to the experience of growing up in an orphanage. I have witnessed firsthand that orphans are not treated the same as others, and this realization has left a lasting impact on me. I internalized the notion that being an orphan would hinder my ability to achieve anything meaningful in life, and this belief is something that I am continually uprooting and healing from.

There were times when I would sit and think about why I didn't have a boyfriend, attributing it to being an orphan who couldn't offer the same experiences as others. The thought of not having a mother and father to walk me down the aisle on my wedding day was painful and left me questioning my true identity.

The message I want to convey to fellow orphans is this: Do not allow thoughts like this to consume you, for you are loved by God, and that is what truly matters. The thought of it may hurt, but remember that it is not the end, and God has your back. Although I despised being an orphan, I now realize that it has shaped me into the person I am now. As an orphan, the best thing you can do is learn to love yourself and be intentional about understanding your identity so you can be proud of who you are.

Living in Haiti made it worse to be an orphan because our government didn't provide much funding or assistance. The worse part was being sheltered in the orphanage for so long, completely detached from Haitian culture and lacking the knowledge necessary to navigate life outside those walls. Hearing others repeatedly declare that we were nothing more than orphans who would never amount to anything was heart-wrenching. It was like the world perceived us as insignificant. What's even more ridiculous is that sometimes people would come behind us and pull our clothes to see what number was on the inside. It made us question whether we would ever be somebody in this world where we were treated like nothing.

Know that being an orphan does not diminish your value or significance in this world. There are people who have both parents but still feel like orphans, experiencing their own feelings of abandonment. We are strong, and God has shaped us to lift others who may have their parents but fail to appreciate them. We can teach them gratitude because there are people who have neither parents nor family, yet they survive. Do not give up and remember that you are not in this struggle alone. We are in this together.

At times, I have questioned if I am worth fighting for or if I hold enough importance in the lives of those around me. There have been moments when I felt like I am not even enough for myself. I have often wondered why I am still alive if there seems to be nothing for me on this earth. The absence of a mother and a father, who are typically a source of comfort for a child, left me feeling lost. What could possibly be expected of me??

I used to perceive my circumstances as something that was slowly destroying me, leaving me with nothing but myself. However, God has shown me that I was never alone. It is truly amazing to know that I am here solely because of Him. While I may not always appreciate this fact, especially when the pain from my past feels overwhelmingly real, I have come to understand that it is okay not to be okay. Sometimes, words fail to capture the depth of emotion I experience just by uttering the word "orphan." It has the power to bring me to tears.

God has revealed to me that being an orphan does not signify the end of my story. He has a purpose in mind for me—to become a mother figure to those who lack one. My question to God was how I could fulfill that role when I myself was raised without the love of a mother? In response, He told me that He was preparing me, and indeed He has been faithful in that regard. I have learned that the path my life has taken is not a result of mere chance; it is because God sees beyond the present and has a vision for my future.

Remember, you are not alone in your struggles. God is with you, guiding and shaping your life for a greater purpose. Your experiences as an orphan have meaning, and there is a reason for the path you have walked. Trust in His plan and hold onto the knowledge that He sees what lies ahead for you.

Family Is Not About Blood

Growing up, I didn't have a traditional family except for the children in the orphanage and the Americans who would come and visit us, along with my schoolmates. I considered them my family. At first, I was hurt that I didn't have blood relatives coming to see me at the orphanage, but now I realize that I have family all over the world.

Family is not defined by blood alone. Anyone who loves you as their own and would do anything to see you happy is family. You don't need a blood connection to call someone family because you may have people all around you who treat you better than your own blood relatives. This is an extra blessing from God because He loves you deeply.

I never thought that people outside of my blood family could become more important than my own relatives until I experienced the love of a mother figure and many others who simply wanted to see me happy. These are the kind of family members that we were meant to have.

Not everyone will love you unconditionally, but when you find someone who would sacrifice their own life for you, that love transcends mere family ties. When something is more significant than the concept of family, that's what they are to you.

I never thought I would truly understand anything about family because I didn't have it while growing up. However, as soon as I left the orphanage, I realized that those children were my family, and they gave me something I never expected to receive from anyone—time and love. I didn't feel deserving of it, but they shared it with me.

I always lived as if I was never enough, giving so much of myself without expecting anything in return, and people took advantage of that. I didn't mind because I felt inadequate. Even now, I still feel like I'm not enough, but I know that there are people who care for me, and I care deeply for them too.

If you ever feel like you're not worthy of love and having a family beyond blood relations, remember that it is possible for God to work it out for you.. At this point in my life, I wouldn't have any family if it were solely based on blood connections. Sometimes it's just hard to believe that some people will accept you into their lives and make you feel loved without any conditions.

You may question your sense of belonging but know that you will never feel that with your heavenly Father. He is the one who chooses the people and places them in your life. They will act as vessels of God's love, making you feel like they are your true family. Also, keep I mind that some people who share the same blood may not consider themselves family.

The Power Of Prayer & Forgiveness
Prayer has the power to bring happiness, but there are times when God is teaching us patience when we struggle during our waiting season. Prayer is something that you may not fully understand until you possesses faith and patience.

There was a time when my daily routine involved waking up at 5:00AM to do rooftop prayers, where I would ask God for happiness and miracles. It was hard waiting for God, but ultimately, my prayers opened many doors as my life progressed. Even when I didn't see immediate results, I continued to pray persistently and pour out my heart to God…even if I seemed like a crazy woman as I cried for the things I thought I would never get.

Repeating this process, I held onto the belief that things would happen, even though I didn't know when it would actually happen. Deep down, doubt would cripple me and make me question whether my prayers would be answered.

At times, prayer can be annoying because we are directing our words to someone we can't even see and sometimes may even doubt exists. The truth is, God does exist, and He is the creator of this beautiful earth. Prayer can also be disappointing, especially when you have prayed for years without seeing any change. But you can't allow that to make you give up.

God's timing is perfect, and He always acts at the right moment. Keep praying and maintain your faith, knowing that things will play out according to God's plan, and in His perfect timing. There are still unanswered prayers in my life, but I cannot give up.

If you go to pray, and find that you don't have the words, know that your tears are a prayer. They are a message that God understands. Know that God hears you. He will act at the right moment, so do not lose hope.

Forgiveness is often misunderstood. Many of us believe that saying "I'm sorry" is enough to seek forgiveness. However, true forgiveness goes beyond mere words. It is a personal process that stems from recognizing the wrongfulness of our actions, feeling remorse, and genuinely seeking forgiveness.

Forcing someone to ask for forgiveness is not a healthy approach because it doesn't come from the heart. I personally struggled with this concept for a long time. I would say I forgave someone, yet the memory of their actions lingered in my mind. It was especially challenging when I had to be around that person all the time.

In the moments of pain I experienced at the orphanage, the adults would come to me and apologize because they knew they had made me angry. But I could sense that their apologies were empty words only being said in an attempt to make me feel better.

I ended up adopting the same behavior: Falsely seeking forgiveness just to make myself feel better. In my soul, I knew this wasn't right. Bitterness consumed me because those superficial apologies didn't fix anything. Reality is, it was the norm in that environment.

I came to a point when I realized the importance of authentic forgiveness. I started to show others that seeking forgiveness meant more than just saying "I'm sorry" and then repeating the same behavior. True forgiveness requires conviction and a commitment to change.

Forgiving someone can be difficult because it requires humility. In a world that often encourages pride, it can be challenging to put our egos aside and ask for forgiveness. However, forgiveness is not a reflection of who holds the highest standard. It is an expression of a big heart and respect for others.

Forgiveness has a transformative impact on our lives. At times, I would refuse to apologize and ask for forgiveness because I didn't feel like the other person deserved my apology…even though I was guilty. It didn't matter how I felt about it, though. This isn't how God teaches us to represent Him.

To truly forgive, we must not only seek forgiveness but also let go of any feelings of superiority or resentment towards the other person. We must forgive and move forward. Moving on is not easy, but it is possible. It requires us to get back on track and not dwell on the past as I once did.

Remember, forgiveness is a journey of the heart, and through it, we can find healing, freedom, and the ability to embrace a brighter future.

Lessons & Blessings
I used to think that people in Haiti, like me, were not blessed because we lacked material possessions and struggled to even afford basic things. When I looked at the lives of people in

different places, I realized that we are all blessed in our own ways. Sometimes we are too busy looking at what we don't have instead of being grateful for what we do have.

Being an orphan has a way of making you question whether you are blessed. You must know that you are blessed no matter what happens. I remember spending a lot of time trying to figure things out rather than being grateful to God for the blessings I did have. It is easy to overlook our blessings when we focus on what we don't have or on things that don't really concern us.

During my time at the orphanage, I believed I was the unluckiest one because I was a true orphan, while some of the other kids still had one of their parents. Growing up there, I thought I wasn't blessed because God had taken both of my parents and the rest of my family, whom I never even knew or had a relationship with.

As I reflect on my life now, I realize that I am close to people I have met along the way. I am grateful for each person in my life, and their presence brings me joy. In fact, I don't even want to hear anything negative about them because I feel so blessed to have them by my side.

As I continue my journey, I have come to believe that I am the biggest blessing to myself. I recognize my worth and the positive impact I can have on others. And now, I want you to understand that you are a blessing too. You are not only a blessing, but you are the blessing.

I am fully aware of how blessed I am at this moment. I know it deep in my heart. I feel chosen, like I have been specially blessed by God. He has granted me numerous achievements that I never thought possible. He did this to show me that I am blessed, regardless of what I go through. He has my back.

Even when I was an orphan, God was there, blessing me with great things. And if He can bless me in that situation, imagine what He can do for you. Even if you seem to have everything you want, but doubt the blessings in your life, know that God is capable of doing even greater things for you.

Looking back on all the things God has done for me, I am so grateful. He helped me come to the state I am in now, which I never thought I could achieve. He has been a tremendous father figure to me, always reminding me of how blessed I am. I no longer have to wish for things because God knows my desires and how truly blessed I am.

Every day, just the act of breathing is a tremendous blessing to me. We often take these simple things for granted, like waking up in the morning, having a cup of coffee, or even having a toothbrush to brush our teeth. These are the blessings we overlook without realizing it.

Remember, it's important to acknowledge and appreciate your blessings every day. Repeat it to yourself, let it resonate within you, and you will see a difference in your life. No matter how little you may possess, you are still blessed. Some would give anything just to have the opportunity to be alive today. Don't take this life for granted, and do not complain. You have more than you know.

CHAPTER 3:

FAITH, LOVE & PEACE

I feel that if I start talking and don't bring up faith, it just doesn't make any sense. I have learned that faith has to be the foundation in order to navigate the challenges of life and persevere. It has both tested me and provided peace in many ways.

Now, you may wonder how I can claim that my faith has tested me, considering that faith is not a person. Let me explain: Faith has pushed me beyond my limits by placing me in situations I believed I couldn't handle. But it is through faith that I was able to overcome those same challenges. In each situation, even when my faith was limited, it played an important part in my ability to move forward, but not without me complaining.

I must admit, I used to be a big complainer, especially when I believed I was right and nothing could change my mind.

However, faith works differently. It requires that we humble ourselves. Having faith in something bigger than us is important because once we possess it, there's no turning back.

When faced with moments of doubt and the feeling that I can't go on, my faith sparks a battle within my mind. I hear two distinct voices—the voice urging me to give up and the voice asking if I'm truly willing to give up. This internal struggle shows that my faith lives within me, beyond my conscious control.

My journey has been filled with moments where I struggled with faith. From having the faith to leave the orphanage, securing my visa on the first attempt, completing my education, to fulfilling my dreams, every step has required a lot of faith. Faith is something I try to understand, but I acknowledge that it is something that goes beyond intellect. I just know that it has led me to where I am now. Though faith sometimes makes things feel harder, I hold on to the belief that what I hope for will come to pass, even if the timing is not what I expect.

In the upcoming chapters of this book, I will talk more about how faith has changed my life. I know it sounds weird, but I encourage you to have faith in faith itself. It takes someone who has endured challenges to really understand how faith can bring about the changes we desire. I have learned that I can't just have faith in myself to accomplish things in my surroundings; I have faith that God can transform anyone, starting from scratch.

As long as you maintain faith in whatever you undertake, you will find yourself aligned with the plan that has been designed for you. Trust that you will reach your destination at the right moment, guided by the faith within you.

Love is a word that none of us can truly define because it

encompasses so much. I've tried to uncover the mystery and understand what makes it so amazing, but it's a word that defies translation. Only God alone can truly know how to define and translate love. However, let me share my personal understanding of love and what it means to me.

Love is the biggest and most cherished word in my vocabulary. I LOVE love, and I'll do anything under its gracious influence. The phrase "love never fails" has become my mantra, giving me strength that no one else could provide. I live my life under the shelter of love, even though love can also bring suffering. I'm willing to endure anything for the sake of love.

Love leads me down paths I never thought I would go, not even in my wildest dreams. It has the power to lift me up to heights unreachable by anyone else. I am where I am today because of love. I am chosen, loved, and favored because of love.

Love plays a great role in my life, and I embrace it wholeheartedly. Love has taught me to find myself, to be patient, and to prioritize others over myself. It has shown me the importance of allowing others to go first, while I am content to go last. And when love fades, I have the strength to start over rather than dwelling on the past.

Love helps me discern between what I truly need and what I merely want. It has revealed to me the true meaning of life, for without love, life would lose its essence. Love extends far beyond romantic relationships; it possesses a depth that encompasses every aspect of our existence.

Love has the power to heal our pain and even cure seemingly incurable ailments. When you have love within you, everything becomes easier and more attainable, even if they appear difficult or impossible at first. But there's a special quality about love that can only be understood by falling in love with LOVE itself.

Love turns nothing into something, it turns the impossible into the possible, and turns your dreams into reality. My dreams were once just fantasies, but now I find myself living them. If I can bring my dreams to life, so can you.

However, embracing love is not always easy. It requires loving those who may not love you, caring for those who may not care for you, being there for those who may not show up for you, praying for those who may not pray for you, and thinking about those who may not even acknowledge our existence. Love demands strength, as it can take you places you didn't want to be, just to change lives you had no desire to change.

You don't have to be loved by others to experience love. Even when your stories leave you heartbroken, the love within you can make it seem like you're fine until you find the strength to heal your scars. No matter how many scars you carry, never give up on love. And always remember that even if you may not feel loved by humans, you are deeply loved by the most high GOD.

Having peace is a beautiful experience. It is the epitome of tranquility and the ultimate state of being. When we face struggles and challenges, peace is the perfect antidote, and there's only one way to obtain it. I can say with full confidence that God alone is the sole provider of peace. Sometimes when we go through trials, we may struggle to find inner peace, but God is the unlimited source.

It's important not to confuse joy with peace. Joy is a feeling of happiness, but peace is having a calm and tranquil mind. It's about not being affected by problems, scars, violence, or insecurities. It's about being able to relax because you possess a soul filled with golden tranquility, and you know that God is in control.

When you have peace, you release your concerns and allow God to just be in control. If you're unsure how to find peace because you've been through a lot, I can offer you what I've learned through my own life story and struggles.

In the past, I lacked peace because I would constantly complain about everything. I would keep replaying the hurt and grievances in my mind, which was a terrible cycle. I held onto things, especially when I was the one who had been hurt, and it only caused more pain. I became consumed with anger towards myself without even realizing it. Meanwhile, the other person had found peace, asked for forgiveness, and moved on, while I remained stuck, clinging to the past.

I never knew how wonderful it felt to have peace until I learned the power of forgiveness and letting go. Forgiving and moving forward is the key that opens the door to peace. Once you possess the key, finding the door and unlocking it becomes a relatively simple task. You make peace your number one priority. Another thing is that peace and love go hand in hand. You cannot claim to have love without having peace within you. Likewise, you cannot say you have peace without the ability to forgive and let go, allowing yourself to move forward.

Now, I can proudly declare that I have peace, and nothing can take it from me. Having peace in my life has taught me to love deeply. It has allowed me to love more intensely. Peace has taught me how to discover and embrace love, and it will do the same for you if you allow it. Embrace peace, let go of the past, and experience the transformative power of love.

CHAPTER 4:

DESTINED TO BE

As I read through my journals, I am astounded by what I have written. It's incredible to see my current life aligning with the words I've written down. It's amazing to see things go the way God had planned them in my mind long ago.

Today, I am realizing that everything transpiring in our lives has already been spoken and set into motion, even if we haven't fully grasped it yet. Our minds are limited, and often God shows us things without us comprehending His message until things unfold. So, let me tell you something: It was destined to be.

Some people don't believe in destiny, but I'm telling you, it's real. And when something is destined to be, there is nothing we can do to change it. We must endure the trials and tribulations we face. The feeling of destiny is often present within us, but we lack the faith to truly believe in it. We sometimes go through challenges knowing that we have to go through them, but still react in ways that are contrary to the knowledge that it was destined to be.

I don't really know how to explain it, but it feels good writing about the concept of "destined to be." Even my experience as an orphan, which I didn't like, was destined to be. Leaving the orphanage was destined to be. So, please understand that nothing in life is a mistake; it is all destined to be. You may not understand it right now, but it is.

I tried writing my book several times, but I know it was God's way of telling me to wait. At that time, there were other things that I needed to write about. I'm actually glad my devices wouldn't allow me to. And guess what? It was all destined to be.

"Destined to be" means that something will happen at the perfect moment, leaving you shocked when it does. I am so proud that my life story was destined to be the way it is. All the pain, all the good times, were destined to be as they are. And I, myself, am destined to be me. Be true to yourself and be proud, for you are destined to be who you are right now.

Not everyone can have the faith to know they are "destined to be" because of all they've been through. But today is the day for you to let it go and know that your life was destined to play out the way it is. Even if you don't believe it yet, soon you will. You are destined for greatness.

You Were Chosen

Jeremiah 29:11 reminds us that we were chosen even before we were born, and we are special and perfect in God's eyes. Being chosen is not a small matter. Each of us is chosen, but it's up to us to embrace and understand our significance. If we don't believe that we are chosen, we won't see ourselves as special to others. In the orphanage, we were constantly told that we were chosen by God to be there, and we questioned why us and not others. Eventually, we learned that everyone is chosen for different purposes.

Whether we like it or not, we are chosen, and we need to believe in it. Even if we can't see the reason at the moment, being chosen means that we are set apart by God for a specific purpose. We need to be prepared for the tasks He gives us. As chosen ones, we are forgiven by God and sometimes have to go through difficult times to teach others how to overcome their own suffering. Life may be simple yet challenging, but once we realize we are chosen, we see things differently and understand our duty to endure hardships. When God chooses us, we are guided through this life journey.

Personally, I was lost and unaware of who I truly was, but God elevated me to a level I couldn't have reached on my own. It's amazing to be where I am now. Therefore, we should rise up and show the world who we truly are as the chosen ones we were meant to be. We cannot change the fact that we are chosen. So, from now on, embrace the truth that you are chosen.

Overcoming the Devil's Hook

Sometimes in my life, when I'm trying to find my way to God, it feels like the devil has placed a fishing hook in my forehead. Every time I start getting closer to God and growing stronger, he pulls me back towards him. It's as if he doesn't want me to be free from his grasp.

With each pull, the hook causes more damage and creates a bigger hole. When you finally break free, you must deal with the healing process. Every time you get triggered, you're reminded of the scar, which sometimes makes it difficult to heal. I allowed myself to be caught in this cycle for a while, believing that I belonged there and that I wasn't good enough to be released from the hook. But deep down, I knew that wasn't where I truly belonged.

Eventually, I realized that I was never meant to be trapped by the devil's hook. I made the decision to let the hook do the damage it was going to do, with the understanding that healing would come in time. I had those holes and scars for a long time. Sometimes it didn't bother me, but sometimes it hurt just enough to make me forget my real identity.

I want to remind you not to let the hook make you forget who you are and what you were born to do. If you do allow it, it may result in you ending up in a space where you won't remember your identity and purpose. The hook has a tendency to make the pain run so deep, that you become addicted to the attention you get from being in pain. It has a way of making you replay your mistakes in your mind over and over, causing you to not only lose sight of yourself, but make you feel unworthy. It can then make it hard to let go of the past.

For a long time, I felt the pain of that hook in my forehead, constantly reminding me of my mistakes and making me believe I wasn't good enough to shine or be truly amazing. But I persisted and kept trying to break free. It was a struggle, and it left a significant hole within me that made me doubt myself. I would get to a point where I had pulled away to get just close enough to reach out and touch the hand of the Father, but the devil would pull me right back. I didn't give up, and I was able to break free, but not without a big hole that caused me to think less of myself.

A few years ago, I took part in a life house skit where I played the role of a human who had turned away from God and was doing what the devil wanted. When I realized that God still wanted me, I attempted to return to Him. The devil fought to keep me from reaching God making it difficult to find my way back and regain purity.

I lost many things in my pursuit to return to God, and it

was a journey full of suffering. I felt the weight of my mistakes and didn't have the strength to find my way back, but it was in those moments that God stepped in and everything changed.

I want to emphasize that none of us are perfect. We all make mistakes, and sometimes we follow paths that lead us away from God. But the beauty lies in the fact that God's love and forgiveness are always there, ready to guide us back onto the right path. The scars and holes we carry serve as reminders of our journey and the strength it took to overcome the devil's hold.

Remember, you are not defined by your past or the scars you bear. You have the power to break free from the hook and embrace your true identity. Let go of the doubts and fears, and trust that God's love will guide you towards the person you were meant to be.

You Are Worth It

We often doubt ourselves and struggle to recognize our own worth. From this day forward, I want you to remember that you are worth it. Sometimes we might feel overwhelmed and doubt ourselves because of the pressure we experience, and this causes us to lose sight of who we truly are. But it's important to know that you are valuable and perfect just the way you are.

Even if what you're doing right now isn't ideal or you recognize it as a mistake, remember that you are accepted and deserving of love. In this journey, you will encounter people who try to undermine you and diminish your worth, but it's crucial to believe in yourself and know that you are truly deserving. Don't let anyone convince you otherwise.

We are not vessels of the enemy, we are vessels for God. We are cherished and loved. It's important to understand that only one person has the authority to determine our value, and that is the Almighty. God loves you deeply and will never intentionally hurt your feelings or tell you things that aren't true.

I've faced people trying to put me down and devalue my worth, but I refuse to accept their lies. Instead, I confidently declare that I am made by God and my worth is rooted in Him. Words hold great power, and it can be painful when people say hurtful things. However, it's essential to remember your true identity and believe in your capabilities. Just as God came to Earth and was rejected by many, yet his true identity prevailed, the same goes for you. Along your journey, you will encounter people who attempt to define you and dictate your worth, but ultimately, it's up to you to know and embrace your true value.

Sometimes, our insecurities arise from past scars, making us feel unworthy. However, it's important to understand that your scars do not define you. From this moment forward, know that you are worth it, and there is nothing that can change that.

You Are A Miracle
No matter what happens to you, it's important to understand that you are a miracle. The fact that you were born makes you a miracle, whether you acknowledge it or not. Being a miracle means that you are a blessing to someone who holds a special place in their heart for you. Not everyone in this life will like you, but those who are meant to be in your life will love you.

From the moment I entered this world, I was a miracle, even though I didn't realize it until much later in life. Some of you may have experienced the pain of being abandoned by your parents at the hospital because they couldn't care for you or because they prioritized other things over you, such as completing their education. But let me tell you, despite any hurtful circumstances, you are still a miracle, and I'll explain why.

You are a miracle simply because you were born. Not everyone who starts the journey of life gets to continue it. You are part of the fortunate ones who are alive, and that in itself is a miracle. You might feel immense pain when you learn about the circumstances of your birth but remember that you are not insignificant. You are everything and a miracle from above.

We often doubt our own miraculous nature, but there's a reason for it. We tend to associate miracles with extraordinary events that happen around us, but we overlook the fact that we ourselves are miracles. Consider this: What if your mother had chosen to have an abortion? What if she had decided not to have any more children? What if your father abandoned your mother, leaving her no choice but to leave you behind? Or what if your mother had struggled with infertility, and yet you were born against the odds? Despite all these possibilities, you are still a miracle, and even if you can't fully grasp it now, one day you'll understand the reason for your existence.

As someone who didn't know either of my parents or have any family and ended up in an orphanage, I too questioned my worth and wondered if I was a mistake. I know many of us ask ourselves why we're alive when it feels like no one cares or we experience so much pain. We may feel lost, unable to find a reason to keep going. But let me tell you, it's because you are a miracle. You are special.

Miracles are always extraordinary and precious, and you are no exception. You are a unique miracle because you are the only "you" in the world. Embrace your individuality because it is what makes you special and remarkable. You can't escape yourself because you are the miracle. It's not something you earn or can discard when you feel like it. It is part of you, even if you struggle to recognize it.

I don't know if you have experienced this, but I often find

that as I'm going through the darkest times in my life, there's a small, deep voice within me that reminds me of who I am. I ponder on why God took my parents away before I even knew them, and I feel sadness, questioning if I'll ever amount to anything or if there will be anyone to celebrate my successes. But that little voice reassures me, saying, "Carmenta, you are a miracle, and there's nothing you can do about it."

You are special, with all your scars and imperfections. You have been chosen and loved by many. Remember, you are a miracle. Don't allow your past or the challenges you've faced to diminish your understanding of your own wonderful nature. Embrace your uniqueness and know that your scars are what make you beautiful. You are chosen.

There is nothing you can do to change the fact that God has proclaimed you as His miracle worker. So, embrace your role and walk forward knowing that you are a miracle, chosen for something extraordinary.

CHAPTER 5:

THE JOURNEY OF PERSONAL DEVELOPMENT

Having an attitude can demonstrate a strong will, but if it is a bad attitude, it can be uncontrollable and cause damage. Growing up, I had a strong and negative attitude, and now I regret not using it for good. My attitude was so strong and negative that the leaders would yell at me, telling me how bad it was. It would provoke reactions from them, and I would intentionally worsen it to elicit further response. That's the power that attitude holds over us—it can control our actions and make situations worse.

As I matured, I began to recognize that I had a bad attitude, but I loved it because it was my only defense when I was mad at the leaders. They probably felt like slapping me but wouldn't do it because I was always around the other children, and they didn't want to instill fear in them. However, as I grew older, I realized the negativity of my attitude and started feeling guilty whenever I acted poorly.

The truth is, when I initially adopted this behavior, I didn't realize what I was doing. Sometimes, in the middle of a conversation, I would realize that I had a bad attitude, but I continued with it. I could have turned that bad attitude into a good one, but all of it became lessons that helped me grow, which I can share now.

The year I was about to turn 11, a significant earthquake occurred, and new children arrived at the orphanage. It was during this time that I began teaching Bible classes and English. This was the time frame when I realized that my bad attitude was not something I really wanted. As a teacher, I couldn't act that way in front of the children while trying to guide them on how to behave. From 2010 to 2017, I taught children wherever I went and became involved in their lives. Some of the children at the orphanage displayed the same bad attitude that I once had, and I knew how to handle them because I had been in their shoes.

All the things we often consider to be mistakes are not really mistakes; they are preparing us for the future. The reality is, I still have both a good and bad attitude within me. The attitude that someone experiences depends on how I am treated. When a friend or a child displays a bad attitude towards you, it is not necessarily a bad thing. Sometimes, it's best to remain quiet and allow them to be, or simply ignore their behavior. Eventually, they may realize their behavior and come to seek forgiveness.

Due to my own attitude, I have learned many lessons, such as how to calm down and be silent. In fact, I've become hesitant to speak sometimes because I fear that my bad attitude may resurface, leading to me becoming angry with myself. Having a bad attitude may make you feel powerful or like you are a leader, but this is an illusion. It ultimately leads you nowhere. On the other hand, having a good attitude allows you to accomplish your goals, remain calm, and be admirable to others.

Attitude is a small thing that can make a big difference. Having a bad attitude was harsh, and discovering its negative impact was even worse because I struggled to control it. It got me into a lot of trouble, including fights and arguments. For a long time, I took pride in my attitude, until I realized that it was destroying me from within, like an addictive drug. It became a tool I relied on to prove that I was a human being too. Now, I understand that it was not good at all, but I also recognize that it was okay to be that way because these are the moments that show that we are all humans who make mistakes that we will eventually regret.

Showing Up For Yourself
In life, it's important to show up for yourself, even when others doubt you. Don't let anyone convince you that it's not worth showing up. Showing up for yourself holds great value.

We often underestimate the impact of showing up because we perceive ourselves as insignificant. We may question why we should show up in reality if we can't even show up for our dreams. However, showing up is worth it. Believe in your ability to show up, and you will see things you've never seen before.

Sometimes, you need to disregard others' opinions and simply show up. The perception people have of you doesn't define your true essence. Deep inside, there's hidden strength waiting to be unleashed. Push yourself and ignore what others say to discover that inner strength.

Showing up is also an act of faith. It's about taking a step that no one believes you can take. There will be moments when you question why you should continue showing up for your dreams or your career, knowing that if you don't, no one else will. But the game is in your hands, and you must show up.

Throughout my life, I've been told I'll never amount to being more than an orphan. However, I consistently showed up for myself, not always expecting blessings but rather standing up for who I am. When people tell you that you can't achieve something, prove them wrong and demonstrate that you are more than they think.

I've realized that showing up is the very thing that can change your life forever. It's an act of faith that shatters the belief that you're not enough. Start showing up in meetings, for your children, at family dinners, and for the things that seem small because they do matter.

Have they told you that you'll never become a lawyer, a doctor, a successful business owner, or become more than they are? Well, it's time for you to show up. You need to show up because if you don't, no one else will do it for you. Simply show up with faith, and everything else will fall into place.

If I hadn't shown up for myself, I never would have reached where I am today. I remember someone who raised me telling me that I would ruin the lives of others, but I had to stand up and show up for myself because no one else would do it for me. I was told I would never amount to anything, but I showed up every morning when God called me. I showed up whenever I was needed, even by those who hurt me and put me down.

All you need to do is show up for the assignments given to you. Your life depends on it.

Overcoming Abuse

Have you ever experienced abuse? If so, it's important to understand that it's not your fault and you shouldn't feel bad about yourself or believe that you're worth any less. I have personally been a victim of mental abuse. Abuse is something that many people, especially girls, go through but often feel ashamed of.

Abuse doesn't necessarily involve sexual acts. It can also be inflicted morally and physically. Physical abuse can take different forms, such as forcing someone to do something against their will, knowing it will harm them in the long run. Mental abuse occurs when someone gives you harmful advice, knowing it will have negative consequences, like advising someone to smoke despite the health risks. Abuse can even be in the form of hurtful words spoken to you.

Before I share my story, I want to encourage anyone who has experienced abuse and is reading this. Remember, no one knows you better than you, and if you understand yourself well, you have the power to change your situation. Mistakes are a part of life, and we cannot undo them.

I have been through abuse, and I have friends who have also experienced abuse, although the types may be different. Regardless of the specific circumstances, it's all classified as abuse. Let me share one story from my time at the orphanage.

I often did things that others couldn't. There was an incident where we asked one of the leaders if we could use nail polish remover because we were running late for a party. We put it in a box with some toys and forgot about it. It was an innocent mistake. Later, when they were going through the toys to give us new ones, the leader found the remover in the box. She was very angry and went off on us, making accusations. The other girls were upset, but being someone who always spoke up, I stood up for all of us. I told her not to speak to us that way, that we hadn't stolen anything and would never do such a thing. She became even angrier, and I was punished for standing up for myself. She even told me that I would ruin all the kids' lives.

That day, I was deeply hurt, and I cried a lot. I couldn't stop thinking about it. It's one of those instances of verbal abuse that still lingers in my memory. Abuse is difficult to forget. I know some of you may have experienced abuse where you were forced to do something against your will. I want to tell you that it's not the end, and you are loved no matter what. Don't let the abuse control who you want to become. You can still achieve your dreams and goals. God can transform victims into victorious warriors, and remember, you are a warrior, scars and all.

Those who have been mentally abused often find themselves constantly apologizing because they're used to excessive criticism. They hide their feelings because they've been blamed for having them. They may break down during minor disagreements because it reminds them of past instances when their abuser exploded unexpectedly. They may need a lot of reassurance because they've been constantly told they're not good enough. To those who have experienced mental abuse, be patient with yourselves. You have the strength to achieve many incredible things.

I had an experience where the employees were told to stop talking to me, although they were supposed to be caring for me. It made me feel like I was worthless, just a disgusting human being. It was a form of abuse that left a lasting mark on me. Even now, the thought of all the hurtful things said to me still hurt. They affect me in the way of making me doubt myself, and sometimes even affecting my self-worth.

I know the answer to that question is yes. The journey of healing has led me to the understanding to know allow these thoughts to take hold, because I am more than enough, even when my mind takes me back to a place I never wanted to be. I encourage you with the same lesson. You can still become the person you aspire to be, with all your cracks, scars, and flaws that you carry throughout your life.

Working Through Confusion

Do you ever feel confused? Life can be complicated at times, so it's not uncommon to experience confusion. We sometimes feel confused when we don't know which way to go or what to do with our lives. Personally, I have experienced moments of great confusion in my life, for the same reason, but also as a result of not knowing who I am.

Feelings of confusion can sometimes lead to making poor choices because we don't know what to do and end up making decisions without clear direction. Confusion can cause us to veer off the right path. Let me share a personal story about how I lost my way due to confusion about what I should have done.

Throughout my life, I have often been confused about my choices. I would question whether I really wanted one thing or another, and sometimes, when I made a choice that turned out to be unwise, I would find myself crying over the confusion and regretting not making the right decision. It's natural to feel confused about things; it's part of being human, and we can't change that. We enter into confusion, and there's nothing we can do to change it except become the change ourselves.

In life, confusion can manifest in different ways. It can arise when we have to make a difficult decision and feel overwhelmed by confusion. It can also emerge when we find ourselves stagnant, unsure of what to do with our lives, despite the passing years. I have personally experienced the detrimental effects of confusion on my life, as it caused significant turmoil.

One of the biggest sources of confusion for me was not knowing who I truly am. I would choose to be someone other than my authentic self. I chose to be the heartbroken person, despite having the potential to be a source of love and inspiration. Insecurity about myself led me to choose a path that wasn't aligned with my true identity. Confusion about my desires and whether I was the right fit for those around me further added to my internal struggle.

Feeling confused can be overwhelming, and it's challenging to navigate through it. However, it's important to remember that confusion is a natural part of the human experience. Embracing the confusion and using it as a catalyst for self-reflection can lead us to greater clarity and understanding, helping us align with our true selves and purpose.

Becoming Your Best Self
Would you be the person God called you to be? Would you be willing to endure suffering so that others can have a better life? Would you go through hard times for the sake of a better future? In essence, would you be willing to embrace the fullness of who you were created to be to walk out your purpose?

We often fear being ourselves and end up imitating others, losing sight of our own identity. It is not right to forget who we are in order to be someone else. Believing in yourself allows you to progress in life. I understand that you may have fallen multiple times and feel hesitant to try again. The weight of past failures can be discouraging. But would you be willing to gather the strength to rise once more and pursue your dreams? There will always be people who try to hinder your progress, but would you at least make one more attempt to see where you can end up?

In the face of failure and discouragement, would you find the resilience to remember your true self and keep moving forward? Is this where you will stop, or will you push through and go after what you truly want? Reconnect with your inner self and realize that you can achieve your desires if you believe and take action.

Are you willing to take the next step, even if it means only progressing a little? Will you embrace your true purpose and accomplish what you set out to do? I also had doubts and struggled to accept my true self for a long time. I felt weak and believed I could never be who I was created to be. However, I realized it is never too late. You can still try again, no matter how many times you fall.

So I ask you: Would you try again? Would you be the authentic version of yourself? I want you to know that you can start anew and pursue what you once thought was impossible. Whenever you think it's all over, ask yourself, "Would I?" Trust that the perfect answer will come to you, and the right paths will unfold once you believe and commit to it.

Can you let go of what is holding you back and move forward? The answer is a resounding yes. Will you finally believe in yourself and prevent negativity from clouding your mind and obscuring the things you were meant to be? Remember, you were born to shine brighter than the sun. Will you accept the invitation to radiate your light?

In this final plea, I ask you one more time: Would you release what holds you back so you can soar further ahead? Would you choose to be yourself, unapologetically and wholeheartedly?

CHAPTER 6:

MIRACLES

In 2010, we moved to a different school to ensure that all of us orphans were together. Little did we know that a massive disaster would strike in January of that year. On January 12th, an earthquake occurred, catching everyone off guard.

That day, I remember being in trouble for chewing gum in class, which was not allowed. I was kicked out of the classroom. I was waiting for my teacher to call me back in and when he finally did, it was time to answer questions about what we had been studying. In school at that time, we studied several chapters in a book, and the teacher could ask us questions about anything in the book. If we hesitated or stumbled, to Him it meant we hadn't memorized it well enough. He might give us a second chance or punish us, but we could never tell which he would do.

When the teacher allowed me back in, he chose me to recite

my lessons first. I knew them well, but he still criticized me for being smart yet disobedient for chewing gum. I replied with a dismissive "Yeah." He promptly kicked me out again, claiming I didn't respond to him properly. I left without saying anything hurtful, just repeating my previous response.

Shortly after I went outside and sat in the same spot, I felt the ground begin to shake. Some kids tried to run, but the teachers kept them inside until the shaking intensified, at which point they allowed them to leave. I was able to make it back inside the classroom to grab my backpack before I ran outside.

We all gathered in the schoolyard, talking, and laughing, oblivious to the fact that it wasn't just our location affected, but the entire country of Haiti. Our phones started ringing with people asking if we were okay and safe. It was then that we realized the magnitude of the earthquake and learned that many people had actually died.

Panic set in as we worried about the well-being of those who helped at the orphanage. Soon, a car of missionaries arrived to pick us up. They asked if we were okay, how we felt during the earthquake, and what was going through our minds. We talked and talked, but it was the most terrifying thing I had ever experienced at just nine years old.

I was in fourth grade at the time, and my life could have ended if I had been one of the people who died that day. But God had a plan, not that He didn't have a plan for those who had passed away, but He had hand chosen me to survive. I kept wondering what would have happened if one of us at the orphanage had died. How would we move forward? At that age, I felt that God was saying that He needed us for more adventures in this chaotic and upside-down life. Although I couldn't fully comprehend what it meant to be chosen and set apart for Him alone, I came to understand why things happened the way they did.

We traveled all over, buying food and water, and helping in any way we could. Looking back, being part of the relief efforts was incredible. Despite my age at the time, I felt strong and capable of making a difference. As people cried and sobbed, we were able to bring hope to those who had lost everything. The earthquake had caused severe injuries, with people losing their arms or legs. Sometimes we take things like having arms or legs for granted, meanwhile the people who experience that type of loss learn the magnitude of that type of loss.

We did everything we could to save lives, but it wasn't enough. We provided a little help to each person, but we couldn't fulfill all their needs. The earthquake brought many people back to God. The following Sunday, there wasn't enough space in the church for those who were regular members because of the number of guests who showed up. It was a tragic event, but it brought many to the feet of God. Many of the people came to understand that they were not enduring this tragic event alone. Being in that place helped them to understand that they didn't have to navigate the aftermath without the rest of the community.

Surviving the Crash

May 16, 2013, is a day I'll never forget. I was thirteen and in the 7th grade. Our principal had organized a road trip for the older kids, but I wasn't really excited about it. I didn't care about having fun since I was used to working hard and staying busy. That day when we woke up, the other kids were happy and excited to go on the trip, but I just sat on my bed as I watched them get ready. Unlike them, I didn't have many friends because they thought I was too confident and acted like I deserved special treatment. Sadly, I ended up embodying their perception of me.

I was confident in myself and had no doubt that I could become the most popular kid in school. I wasn't seeking attention; it just seemed to come naturally and I embraced it. However, this led to many people disliking me. Because of this, I wasn't excited about going on the trip. There were other kids who wanted to go with our group at school, and eventually the leaders agreed and paid for us all to attend.

When the day of our trip arrived, I still didn't want to go. One of the caretakers who was watching us tried to encourage me to cheer up and go. "Please, it will be fun!" she said. Reluctantly, I agreed and got dressed.

We always prayed before we left the orphanage. The Director gathered us around to pray, but the kids were so excited and playful that they couldn't focus long enough to be still. This irritated the Director and he threatened us by saying we wouldn't go. I grabbed my iPad to play my music. I would be just fine if that was the case.

The trip was intended to allow us to explore our history, and it turned out to be fun. Suddenly, heavy rain started pouring down, and we all rushed back to the bus. The noise inside the bus combined with the rain made it difficult for the driver to control the vehicle on the slippery road. He repeatedly told the kids to be quiet, but no one listened. After a few minutes, he lost control, and the next thing I knew, we had crashed.

Many people were severely injured, but miraculously, there were no fatalities. The bus could have fallen into a deep river, but instead, it collided with the mountainside, sparing us from a worse outcome. The leaders from another bus quickly came to our aid, attending to the injured and arranging for them to be taken to different hospitals. I was hurt too, but in the midst of the chaos, I didn't feel the pain that day.

As everyone exited the bus, I realized my leggings were torn, and it was then that I discovered a glass had cut my buttock and elbow. It was strange that I hadn't felt it at the time. That day was the most terrifying and painful experience of my life. I had faced death head-on, and the fear I felt made me think I was going to die.

This accident served as a turning point, making me realize the importance of taking life seriously. In just a split second, everything could change, and we could lose what is most precious to us—our lives. When I finally arrived home late that night, we had been searching for one of the kids from the orphanage who had been seriously injured and ended up in a hospital. The caretaker noticed my torn leggings and asked if I was okay. It was then that I realized the extent of my injuries— a painful reminder of the accident.

That day, I had a glimpse of death and it made me value life in a whole new way. I became acutely aware of the fragility of life and the importance of treasuring every moment. This experience taught me not to take life for granted and to live each day to the fullest.

This event gave me a deep sense of gratitude and appreciation for life. I carry the lessons I learned from that accident with me as I journey through life. It reminds me to cherish every moment, never taking life for granted, and embracing each day as the precious gift that it is.

Answered Passport Prayers
In order to travel between Haiti and the United States, I had to get my visa and passport. I went through the application process and was informed after eight days that I should go and collect my passport, and the visa would be inside. At that time, my email wasn't working on my phone, so my mom was logged in on her phone to keep me updated on everything.

I'll never forget when she told me, "Carmen, the visa has been issued. You have to go and get it." I was shocked because

I thought it was supposed to take longer. When I looked at the screenshot she sent me, it clearly showed that it had already been issued. I couldn't believe it had happened so soon.

The following day, my friend Skay was heading to Port-au-Prince, so I asked if I could ride with him so I could go and collect the passport. When I arrived, I realized that I didn't have any information about what I needed to bring with me for the passport pickup. I soon found out that one of the required documents was the paper that was attached to the visa information. It had a confirmation code they needed to verify to my identity.

I handed over my ID when I entered, in hopes that it would be sufficient, but I was denied. I pleaded with the attendant, suggesting they look at the picture on my passport to confirm that it was indeed me with the same name. They insisted that I couldn't have the passport without the required information.

I stepped outside, contemplating how I was going to retrieve the passport. I was far from my house so I didn't have the option to just walk home to get it. Fortunately, there were some people in a car who offered to help. They asked for $20, and I thought, "Yes, I have that," and proceeded to hand them the money. The man clarified that he meant American dollars, not gourdes, which is Haitian currency. I picked up the phone to call Skay and gave him the full story of what was happening. I then asked if he could help me. He came back and took me home to get the documents I needed, then gave me $20 in American dollars. I was ultimately able to return with the required documents and information and they finally handed over my passport.

When I got home, I couldn't stop staring at the visa in my passport. I felt an overwhelming sense of happiness and pride. Nobody could take away this joy from me. I had put in the hard work, and I had succeeded.

During the process, I never doubted it, even once. I knew God would take care of me, and He did. In life, nothing is impossible. The word itself says "I'm possible." So, what are you waiting for? Face your biggest fears and tackle the things they say are difficult to achieve. Never give up because God is with you, and you are not alone.

Slow Miracles

There have been times when I forgot the meaning of my existence and allowed the words of others to deeply affect me. I let them get inside my head and make me believe things I initially rejected. The challenges of life are enough as they are but imagine trying to battle when you feel ill-equipped for the fight. The year 2020 was a personal struggle for me because my case for staying in this country was particularly difficult and complicated.

I remember sharing with someone that I would be extremely busy in the coming months as I made preparations, and she laughed in disbelief. It hurt me deeply because it seemed that they believed miracles could happen to them, but not to me. I was speechless and just processed the hurt in a silent battle. I was determined to emerge triumphant and prove them wrong.

When I was growing up, I constantly heard that I was spoiled just because my life was different from many other Haitians. I began to believe it, until I came to the United States and witnessed how truly spoiled and ungrateful some people can be despite having so much. They made me believe I could never have more than what they offered me, and I held onto that belief for a long time.

Things always seem easy when you're not in the situation or haven't experienced it yourself. Sometimes, even if you have gone through a similar situation, you forget how difficult it truly was. It always appears easy, but in reality, it never is. Even though I'm in the United States now, it's still tough. Everyone thinks and assumes it's easy, which is far from the truth. I would say that it's better and different, but it's certainly not easy.

Sometimes, the way we picture things in our minds makes them seem easy until we step into the actual situation. As a believer, I know that anything is possible as long as you give it a try. However, that doesn't mean the process itself won't be hard. Before coming to the United States, I had a mental image of how things would unfold, but it turned out to be the opposite of what I had envisioned. I never thought it would be difficult because it all seemed easy in my mind, but that wasn't the reality.

I'm currently in the process of applying for asylum and waiting for an answer that remains uncertain. I'm not able to attend college because I don't have my diploma with me. It's still in my home country, where the situation is chaotic and unstable. Now I find myself wondering why I had pictured everything to be so easy in my mind when the reality is much harder to figure out.

CHAPTER 7:

EMBRACING GOD'S PLAN

Living in a new place with new people and experiences doesn't guarantee perfection. I've learned that the perfect time doesn't always align with our own desires but rather with God's plan.

Being in the United States doesn't mean I don't still have struggles. In fact, I often find myself facing more struggles because there are more opportunities and aspirations, but fewer resources to make them a reality. Every morning, I wake up with dreams of who I want to become, but it's disheartening when the timing doesn't seem right and it weighs heavily on my soul.

Observing others who have opportunities and squander them without realizing their value, while I'm in the background trying to make things work, is another challenge. There were moments when I questioned if life in Haiti was better, despite things being upside down because there was something there that seems absent here. Making things happen in the United States feels like an uphill battle, where I have to exert force, but timing doesn't align with my efforts.

To be honest, the reality of what I encountered in the U.S. was not what I expected. It feels like a different world with hidden problems it tries to conceal from outsiders. I can't complain, but it often feels like I'm in a race with my own enemies, because I want them to see that I can succeed without showing any signs of weakness even though I'm struggling internally. It's a battle I fight alone, and no one truly understands. People around me might perceive it as a cakewalk, but once I got to the States, I started to experience depression because all I could do was yearn and want.

Everything I craved was good for my well-being, but I had to learn to wait and allow the right moments to unfold. I tried to maintain a positive outlook, but there were times when I couldn't because I'm not a robot—I have emotions just like anyone else. Life in the United States didn't treat me well in the first few months. I felt so overwhelmed and lost, unsure of how to navigate my new life.

Life in the United States can be tough and complicated at times. It was far from perfect, and everything happening around me felt like it was just too much, gradually chipping away at my spirit. I went through it all and emerged as a warrior, but it wasn't perfect.

Coming to the United States completely threw me off. The only way I can explain it, is it made me feel small. It's difficult to explain, but it was hard. Things seem so easy when they are on your mind until you actually get in possession of whatever it is. Then you realize it was all in your head.

As long as it remains in your head, you can learn to make it though and win in the process. That's how I emerged as a winner—by refusing to let the difficulties define me.

My Last Year of School in Haiti

I am 100% Haitian and proud of my African heritage. Because of my background, sometimes I felt like I would never succeed at anything. It was the result of constantly hearing negative stereotypes about Haitians, like being labeled as thieves. At first, it didn't bother me because I knew I wasn't one of them.

However, as time went on, I couldn't help but feel angry hearing those stereotypes being repeated by Americans at the orphanage. It was disheartening to be made to feel guilty about my nationality and pressured to be someone I wasn't. I've realized that in life, there will always be people who want to mold us into someone we're not, making us feel bad about ourselves and questioning why we were flawed and placed in these circumstances.

But God placed me there to be different, to show the world that I can be a positive representation of my country. Despite the challenges and poverty in Haiti, I believe we are some of the happiest people on Earth. We know how to love deeply, and when we love, we love wholeheartedly. Yes, we make mistakes like everyone else, but that doesn't define us. Our scars are what make us a unique and resilient nation.

Growing up with an American influence, I was often treated like an American, but when I went to school, I faced a different reality. Hearing that I wasn't good enough because of my Haitian identity shattered me, but that didn't stop me from believing that being Haitian is beautiful and amazing. Our nationality doesn't make us bad; it's unfair to generalize and judge us based on the actions of a few. We are a proud and diverse people, and I feel comfortable and proud to be part of the Haitian community.

I've always loved school, in spite of the fact that we have

thirteen grades in Haiti. When I returned to Haiti after my birthday in September of 2018, I was excited to reunite with my friends and embrace my studies. I had only missed one day of school and I was really proud of that. I brought candy and snacks to share with them because giving has always been part of who I am. Sometimes, my giving nature was taken advantage of because I struggled to say no, but I've come to accept that it's how God made me, and I appreciate that aspect of myself.

During those three months in school, I dedicated myself to improving in subjects where I wasn't strong. I worked hard in math and physics and was proud of my progress. As December approached, I couldn't contain my excitement to celebrate Christmas back in the United States. It was my first Christmas there, and the experience was filled with joy. I enjoyed church visits and quality time with friends and family.

During that time, my papa gave me valuable advice to write down my experiences and testimonies. He asked whether I remembered what happened in the process of my transition. I remembered it all. I took his suggestion to heart and started journaling to capture my experiences, though sometimes I'd forget the little details in the busyness of life. I'm so grateful that he used his wisdom to encourage me. It has only made me love him even more.

On January 7th, I returned to Haiti and attended a party with my classmates in philo to celebrate Saint Thomas D'Aquin. In English, it translates to Thomas Aquinas. This was a celebration for everyone in the last grade, similar to how graduations are celebrated in the American culture. We dressed up for a presentation that was about Saint Thomas D'Aquin and enjoyed our time together. I had bought two dresses before I left the states so I could have something to wear.

It was a day filled with laughter and unforgettable memories as my classmates and I spent the day at a hotel. We had lunch, and I ended up being the leader of the games and prizes. Despite the crisis happening in Haiti, we took the risk of going out in a private car. When we encountered roadblocks due to the burning of an office in Montrouis, we didn't let it put a damper on our fun. We screamed and made noise, reveling in the joy of life. People looked at us like we were crazy, but we didn't care.

Those moments of happiness created a stronger bond among us, but then as we spoke about the future we all felt the mood shift, knowing that completing school would mean we would spend less time together. Although we were sad, we vowed to stay connected by phone. I was especially sad because I had a tourist visa but knew I would try to enroll in college in the States.

As I prepared to embark on my college journey in the United States, I remembered that being Haitian is a source of strength and pride. I would carry with me the love, joy, and resilience that defines my culture. Challenges would arise, but I would face them with determination and a positive outlook, knowing that my identity as a Haitian is a gift that sets me apart.

School Testimony
Two weeks after school started, the crisis in Haiti escalated, and it became too dangerous for us was a terrifying time, with people burning tires and engaging in violent acts. The bandits wreaked havoc, targeting banks, stores, and mini markets. We were trapped in our homes, living in fear for our lives. Food was scarce because most of everything in Haiti has to be imported but there were no resources. With things being so volatile, it was pointless anyway because people were carelessly destroying things and it would have just resulted in waste.

In March, we attempted to return to school, despite the

ongoing crisis. All of the children from the orphanage attended the same school. I had a routine of cooking before leaving for school, both to save money and to have food for myself and my friend, Rose. She was in the 8th grade, and we shared a special bond. During breaks, if she didn't come to find me, I would find her.

One day, Rose told me that she had plantains and other vegetables that resembled plantains, along with bananas. She offered them to me, suggesting that I could cook for both of us. Since we shared everything and had a sisterly bond, I accepted her offer. I placed the vegetables and bananas in my bag and brought them home.

The next morning, I woke up early, did my devotion, prayed, then began cooking. I peeled the vegetables and put them in a pot on the stove. I tried turning on the fire but the stove wasn't working properly. I tried several times but couldn't get it to function. Feeling frustrated, I took a shower and went to school.

When I arrived at school, I went straight to class so I wouldn't be late. During the break, Rose asked me about the food I had brought. I explained that my gas had run out, and I would need to buy more after school. She offered to give me money, but I reassured her that it was okay. We bought lunch together, and when school ended, I went back home without buying gas because I had snacks and wasn't very hungry.

Later in the evening, around 5:00, I went to the gym. Afterward, I decided to go to the gas station to check if they had propane, even though the crisis had caused shortages. To my surprise, they said they did have a supply. It made me angry because I had just bought a tank of propane but my stove wasn't working. I confronted them, accusing them of filling my tank with air. The person at the gas station denied it and insisted they would never do such a thing because they knew me. They wouldn't try to do anything like that to me. I told them I would be back to buy the propane, but by the time I got home, I changed my mind. I decided I would go the following day.

When I arrived home, I had some kids over, and we played cards together. I also helped them with their English studies. In the midst of everything, I completely forgot about the pot that I had left on the stove from the previous day. The next morning, while I was praying in the darkness, I heard a voice telling me to check the pot on the stove. I grabbed my phone and turned on the flashlight, uncovering the pot. To my horror, I saw that there were all of these prickly things sticking to the plantains. Fear ran through my veins, and I moved away from the stove. I waited until my mind was clearer and looked at it again, confirming what I had seen.

Terrified, I took a picture of it and showed it to a girl from the orphanage who was in the same grade as me. She was perplexed by it, asking what it was. I then sent the picture to another girl from, asking her to show it to one of the employees to determine what it could be. When she showed the message to her, she said it was poison. I was taken aback by the news. They asked how it could have happened, and I explained the situation, still filled with fear.

During the break, the first thing I asked Rose was whether a particular boy liked her. Confused, she replied, "No, why?" I showed her the picture and asked if he had stolen the plantains. Uncertain of the truth, she agreed not to accept anything from people anymore. It was a chilling realization that people could harbor such hatred towards others.

In that moment, I understood why God had prevented me from buying gas the previous day. That became the testimony of how God had saved my life by preventing me from being poisoned.

The Last Visit

Being a human is challenging because often we have no control over the waiting or the circumstances falling apart around us. It's not up to us, but up to God. All I could do was observe and remain silent, even though I didn't know if this was how God intended to start the process of blessings in my life. But that was how it began, and despite the suffering, I held onto the hope that something better was in store for me. It was difficult to wait without knowing what I was waiting for.

The last time I was visited by the people I had come to know as family, it was a nightmare. I was grounded during the time they were present. It was terrible to be able to see them there without being able to see or talk to them. At that moment, I felt like rebelling and doing things I wasn't supposed to do. I was mad, but I couldn't do anything about it; I had to watch them having fun with the other kids while I stayed in my room, feeling sad. It seemed like the devil had planned it, and God allowed it to test my faith.

Whenever the leaders of the orphanage would find out that some of the other kids talked to me, they would lock me in a hot box. It was a small, empty room that would get unbearably hot, and I had to eat my meals in there too. I couldn't risk speaking up; it would only get me in more trouble.

At the time, I couldn't understand why God would separate me from the people I loved. All I felt was pain and suffering as I was forced to sit back and watch everything unfold. I was devastated, but I had to let it go, knowing that it wasn't my plan to make myself happy but God's plan.

Being a human being is hard sometimes because many things are beyond our control, and we must trust God's timing. The day they left, they said they wouldn't return because of everything that had happened, and it was heartbreaking to hear. I remember as they were leaving, I snuck out to hug them one last time until we met again. The pain and guilt inside me were overwhelming in that moment. I watched them drive away and waved goodbye.

As the truck reached the gate, it stopped for a moment. My Uncle Troy jumped out and ran to hug me. He said goodbye, gave me some money, and told me to find a way and text him if I ever needed anything. He assured me that they all loved me and that they would be back for me. At that moment, I didn't understand why he said those things, considering they had just told all of us that they wouldn't be returning to the orphanage. I was completely bewildered. It was only later, as I began the process of my journey, that everything started falling into place, but not without more challenges. I wanted to leave but wasn't sure how I could.

There was a time when I was a part of the youth leadership team as the secretary. We were involved in various activities with the kids, and we would take turns leading the youth on Sundays. Before leaving, I had different plans for sending my belongings out. My initial idea was to drop them off at someone's house during youth group meetings. However, that plan didn't work out. Then I thought about asking one of the ladies who worked there to carry a few things for me whenever she went home. But soon they started inspecting the bags of the employees, so I didn't want to risk her job or safety.

I also considered giving my belongings to a friend near the back gate by the ocean. However, after praying about it, I didn't feel peace about that option either, and I started to lose trust in her. So, I prayed even more and surrendered the situation to God, telling Him that if it was His plan for me to leave, He would figure it out and show me what to do.

I didn't worry because I knew God was in control of the process, and there was nothing I could do on my own. As the song goes, when Jesus says yes, nobody can say no, and I truly believe that. I couldn't say no because God was leading me down paths that were unseen, and I had to trust and watch Him work alone.

Though I felt alone at times, that's when I began to sense His presence with me. I never gave up on what I had started, and even now, I'm still fighting to reach where I want to be, knowing that with God's power, I can achieve it.

Trying to sneak my things out was challenging, and in the end, I ended up not being able to because it really wasn't part of God's plan. He wanted me to leave like a princess because that's who I am. I had never truly realized my identity as a princess of the Most High God until I started putting the pieces together. Now, I understand that all the things happening in my life are just the beginning of my story and the miracles that await me.

When God says "enough" to something, it truly means it's enough. That's what He showed me. As I surrendered to His plan, everything else started to align. It's not a secret or a fairytale; God made me a winner, and He is still doing things in my life that I never even thought to ask for. As I move forward in life, it often feels like things aren't progressing as quickly as I'd like, but when I look back, I see that God has been working behind the scenes, surprising me with His plans.

I can't find the words to express how immense and merciful His presence is in my life every single day. When I moved to the United States, I felt like life had thrown me a curveball. Being home all the time was a struggle for me. I was used to giving advice, talking, hanging out with friends, and having kids from the orphanage around. But here, everything was different. I couldn't work, couldn't drive myself anywhere, and I didn't have friends. I became even more of a homebody, which made it even more challenging.

I longed to be out there, showing the world who I am, making friends, and feeling free. But it wasn't in God's plan for that to happen right away. That's when God revealed to me that my life would not be a secret. He told me that what I was about to experience would astonish me. That it wasn't a fairytale; it was real.

He spoke to my heart, saying, "You are a pure pearl, and I am going to show the world that it has nothing that can buy you. You are too precious to be assigned a price." My story is not meant to be kept as a secret; it was simply in a safe place until the right time. I realized that my ultimate goal in life wasn't just to accomplish my own desires, but it was to be the miracle that God created for this world.

As a young girl, I began learning how to drive. In Haiti, it wasn't common for girls to drive; it was mostly guys. Coming to the States, I wondered if I would ever be able to drive like the guys. God's answer to me was a resounding "Yes!" He assured me that I would show the world that I am the exception. In my pursuit of becoming a better version of myself, He made it clear that I am enough, even when I doubted it. He proved me wrong and continues to do so.

After my seasonal work at a major membership warehouse club, I worked for a large distributor of industrial tape for a short time. I ended up going back to the warehouse club. Though it was a shorter stint, I believe there's a reason for it that I don't yet understand. Through hard work, juggling multiple jobs like working a regular job, doing hair on the side, and cleaning, I managed to save enough money to buy a car. It's an accomplishment I am incredibly proud of.

Understand that your life is not a secret. The time just hasn't come for you to shine and reveal who you were designed to be. When I look back at everything God has done, from taking me out of my mother's womb and placing me in an orphanage, to bringing me to the United States and giving me a new life, I can't fully comprehend the magnitude of it all. But God keeps telling me that He didn't bring me this far just to leave me here; there is more to come.

Remember, anything God has done for you is not your secret to keep; it belongs to Him. Your task is to let others know that He is able. Although what you have witnessed seems like a fairytale, it is real. I am still processing everything that has happened in my life since day one, and sometimes it feels unreal—too good to be true. But I'm here to tell you that it is true.

Don't give up on sharing your story with the world. Don't be afraid to be the hands and feet of God, and boldly declare that He is more than enough for you. What you choose to show the world about what God has done on your journey is not a dream; it is a reality. One thing I've learned is that it was never my battle to begin with, and it is not my secret to keep.

Birthday Blessings
My mom had rented a house in Haiti for me to live in as I was travelling back and forth between home and the States. Before I left the States to go back to Haiti for the second time, in a conversation with mom, I learned that the lease would be ending soon. She expressed her concerns about raising money for the rent, as well as my school supplies and plane ticket. It was going to be a lot and she needed some support. She had already helped me so much, and I wanted to show her that I could contribute too. I assured her that I would figure it out and raise the money.

I decided to post on Facebook, offering Haitian food, hairstyling services, babysitting, and house cleaning. I made it clear that I wasn't asking for money, but rather providing opportunities for people to help me while giving them something in return. To my surprise, many people stepped up to assist me. I received various small jobs, did people's hair, and babysat. Some even gave more than I expected.

I was incredibly blessed by their support. I sent the first amount of money down to Haiti so they could secure the key for my new house and transfer my belongings. Then, on the following Sunday, I gathered with family and friends. Uncle Troy prayed for me and expressed gratitude to everyone who had helped. I was outside at the coffee bar saying my goodbyes and people continued to bless me. We took the opportunity to invite those who were there to my birthday party. It was such an emotional moment. I was in tears and felt a bit embarrassed as everyone gave me money and hugged me. I was overwhelmed by the love and generosity I experienced.

When I returned home, I was shocked by all the surprises awaiting me. People were there, waiting to welcome me back, and all I could think was, "God is good." We celebrated my birthday, which marked the first time I had a proper party. I had so much fun, dancing like nobody was watching and laughing until I couldn't anymore. It was a truly special day. The money I received completed the remaining amount for the house, and I even had enough left over to buy snacks for my return trip and cover expenses for a couple of months before my mom could send me money.

I also received two bracelets, each with a different meaning. One had the logo of the orphanage I grew up in, which said, "Change a child, change a nation." The other had the phrase "ex.con," symbolizing a person who was once imprisoned but is now free. I interpreted it as being imprisoned by our sins and finding freedom through forgiveness. I wore each bracelet to feel connected to my friends. It was truly an amazing year. All of these gestures meant so much to me, and although I wasn't ready to go back to Haiti, I was determined to make the best of it. I still had one more year of school ahead.

I was also sad about going back to Haiti because I felt a strong sense of belonging. I didn't want to leave my newfound family behind. To share my appreciation for those connections, I have shared some of those stories throughout this book, but at that time, I took the opportunity to write letters to all my friends from my youth. I poured my soul into the words I shared. I don't know if they received it in the same way I intended, but it was the best I could give.

The next day was my birthday. I had a friend who stayed over and we decided to go shopping to have some fun. Later in the day, a special friend named Kashmindal came to visit me. She drove all the way from Kent State just to spend an hour talking to me. I felt so loved by her, and her presence meant the world to me. My birthday that year was filled with kindness and joy.

Early the next morning, I left for Haiti, bringing an end to that momentous trip. It was a journey where I witnessed the hand of God working in my life, reminding me that He never starts something without finishing it.

CHAPTER 8:

LEARNING & GROWING

In this world, there are two realms in particular that coexist that I'd like to talk about—the physical and the spiritual. We don't go back to dig up buried bodies in the physical world, but the same cannot be said for the spiritual realm. In the spiritual dimension, we must be willing to revisit and dig up our old selves when we find ourselves in situations that we were never meant to be in. The we must find and tap into the version of ourselves that carries goodness and authenticity.

The truth is that we often fail to recognize this buried treasure as we have become accustomed to our flawed selves. The false sense of security that accompanies the flawed identity keeps us stagnant, giving us the illusion of progress while we remain trapped.

To break free from these things, we must begin the process of digging. We need to rediscover the parts of ourselves that have long been dormant and unrecognizable even to our own eyes. The world we live in, where others dictate who we are and confine us to predetermined roles, must not define us. This journey of digging up our true selves is necessary for personal growth.

Sometimes we only find pieces of our buried identity, and only choose the pieces that serve us in the present while leaving the rest behind. I have been guilty of selectively digging, haunted by the shame and guilt that hindered me from embracing my entirety. The pain and anguish of digging up those roots are so intense that I question why I would subject myself to such pain. But still, I do it because I understand that there is greater on the other side.

I have become intentional about the pursuit of my true self, understanding that the pain and challenges that come with unearthing my buried identity are necessary for growth and healing. In each attempt, my goal is to reclaim who I am, embracing the goodness and authenticity that were meant to accompany me on this lifelong journey. A lot of times, we allow things to have control over us that shouldn't. We let them bring us down without even realizing it. We carry regrets and wishes for things that could have been different if only we had known better.

Experiencing God's Faithfulness
Throughout my life, God has continuously shown me His unwavering presence and faithfulness, fulfilling His promises to care for me even before my birth. He has always kept his promises.

The process of obtaining the necessary information to apply for my EAD (Employment Authorization Document) seemed like a daunting task, but it was a miracle that it only took a week or two. It was truly a blessing that all my paperwork was processed promptly and arrived precisely when needed.

As I navigated the asylum application, there was a requirement to wait 150 days before applying for employment in the state. On the 150th day, I submitted my EAD papers just in time. They had just updated the process and increased the waiting time to a year. I was so blessed to be able to get mine submitted before they made that change.

The approval process began, and it only took a week to receive my first letter. Every week after that, I received another piece of mail regarding my work permit until I had received all the necessary documents. When God's is working in you, you just have to let Him do what He does best. It's a reminder that He is capable of anything.

I submitted my i765 right before the deadline, eliminating the need to pay any fees. This was another testament to God's work in my life, assuring me that He had never forsaken me, even during moments when I felt alone and unloved. His constant presence was reaffirmed time and again.

There came a point when I changed my address. I was to get a biometrics appointment, which never happened. When I checked my case status online, I discovered that the appointment had been set for October 13th, which had already passed. It appeared that they may have sent notification regarding the appointment to the old address.

I sent a screenshot of the message about the missed appointment to my mother, but she was busy and told me we could talk about it when got home that day. I needed to connect with her. Reading that I had missed the appointment scared me because it meant that I might not get my EAD card. I was finally able to get it, but I still have to wait to apply for my green card.

Often, we are unaware of the blessings God has already prepared for us until the appointed time. These abundant blessings have been an incredible reminder that there is nothing He won't do on my behalf, even if it means I have to walk through fiery trials to achieve the plans He has set before me.

I have faithfully walked through the fire, even when it caused me pain. God's voice continually reminds me that I will come out stronger when I accomplish all that He has assigned me.

I always used to say as I was growing up that we shouldn't wish for things, but rather pray, because we have a God, not a genie. However, as I journeyed through life, I discovered something I never could have imagined. For those of you who may not be familiar with the concept of a genie, it's something that may not be real, but it represents the idea that the person who possesses it can make wishes and have them granted.

But here's what I realized: God is like our genie, except we don't simply make wishes; we pray for what we desire, and it shall be given to us. First, if you have a genie, you're already the master of it. So how can a genie dictate the number of wishes you have when you're the one in control?

It can't. I believe we all have a genie inside of us, but it lies dormant until we awaken it. Once this genie is awakened, it becomes ours to command, and we can give it as many orders as we desire. Because we are the master, our orders are unlimited. Let me break it down further.

The genie represents the belief we have in ourselves. It's something that we can't access until it is awakened, but once we do, we realize that we are capable of achieving anything. The genie resides within us, and we simply need to learn how to bring it forth and direct it towards our desires. However, this can only happen if we truly believe. The genie is like a dormant spirit within us, and once we awaken it, miracles begin to unfold in our lives, surpassing our wildest imaginations.

The genie is YOU—it's the spirit that resides within you, a spirit that may be difficult to comprehend. It's your own inner spirit, the part of you that you may struggle to release. But once you do, all your beliefs and desires shall manifest.

You must get deep into your thoughts, unlocking that spirit and discovering the true essence of who you are. If the genie cannot emerge from the lamp by itself, surely the spirit cannot manifest without your conscious effort.

Summon the strength within you, inspired by the power of God, and tirelessly strive to bring forth your inner genie. It won't be easy, but if you truly desire it, you will attain it. Remember, Aladdin faced numerous challenges before he obtained the lamp, and eventually, he had it in his possession. Now, I challenge you to focus on awakening your inner genie and fight to set it free. It's only your genie that can reveal the true depths of your being.

If your spirit is pure, your genie will reflect that purity, for it is a manifestation of your own spirit and imagination. I have unleashed my genie, and it feels incredible. Now, it's your turn to discover and unleash yours within you.

Twins: Guilt & Shame
One of the biggest killers in my life has been guilt and shame. The feeling that I couldn't make any mistakes or show any flaws, as if I had to be perfect to avoid disappointing others who never truly walked in my shoes. It left me with a constant sense of not being enough, not just for them but even for myself.

Growing up as a Haitian, hearing constant negative

judgments and being made to feel like we were all bad didn't make it any better. Instead, it only built up guilt inside of me. It made me question my worth and made me believe that I would never measure up.

For a long time, I held the misconception that Americans were perfect. Their differences and the idealized image of their country convinced me that they didn't make mistakes, lie, or even experience basic human functions like eating and using the bathroom. But when I discovered that Haitians and Americans were alike in many ways, the guilt intensified. Each truth I learned about the lies only deepened the sense of guilt inside me.

That guilt could have killed me, and no one would have ever known that was the cause of death, because I tried to hide it. It would eat away at me, fill me with anger, and cause me to hide the guilt within, fearing that if I let it out, others will see me differently. It's a painful process to have something slowly killing you from the inside but lacking the strength to release it and free yourself.

Guilt is a destructive force that leaves you with nothing and demands even more. I couldn't understand why I harbored so much anger inside or how to reverse it. I searched for answers but couldn't find them.

Growing up with the belief that I was never good enough was dangerous. It created a mindset that I would never be worthy, regardless of the help or efforts made to show me otherwise. Life seemed to be trapped in a bottle, sealed, and discarded, with no hope for change or rescue from the chaos.

Having guilt inside me made me believe that no one would ever truly need me. However, when I discovered that I had the power to release the guilt, I felt a sense of relief. I know many of you also carry this kind of guilt, not knowing how to let it go because you're stuck in the current state of your life. It feels like there's no way forward or backward. But what you can do is release that guilt and choose yourself.

The only way to conquer guilt is by letting it go, knowing who you are, and believing that you can overcome it. Stop allowing past hurts to continue hurting you today. Embrace the new life and the new you and focus on doing things differently. Guilt can only to destroy you and hold you back as if you don't release it. Choose to break free.

Low Moments

When I find myself feeling down and struggling to understand life, my thoughts become unclear. The phrase "in the dark" accurately describes my state of mind. I feel lost and uncertain, not knowing what path to choose or how to navigate certain aspects of my life. This feeling of being in the dark is overwhelming and disorienting.

Throughout my journey, I've learned that I have the capacity to bring both light and darkness into the world. Just as I can radiate light and positivity, there are times when the darkness within me surfaces. It depends on what I choose to manifest in the world.

I want to emphasize that the place I find myself in is far from perfect. Even when I enter a room, I bring my own darkness with me. It's a part of who I am, and it emerges when I switch off my inner light. My life contains a great deal of darkness that I struggle to comprehend on my own. It becomes overwhelming and difficult to manage, often spiraling out of control.

I recall a moment when I was sitting at a table writing my book. I took a break and started searching online for things I desired in life. I realized that not everything I want will be attainable or provided by my parents. Sometimes, I need to take responsibility and show up for myself. However, during this research, my mind wandered to an alternate world where I tried to make everything fit together.

However, dwelling in overthinking is not productive. It only serves to remind me of where I came from and what my life would be like if I hadn't reached this point. The thoughts continue to swirl endlessly, without resolution.

I have a mentality that pushes me to pursue my desires, even if it means walking through fire. In recent weeks, I've felt a great desire for the whole the world, but I struggle to carry the weight of these ambitions on my shoulders. I understand the importance of patience, but when I wait for too long without any progress, I can't help but feel responsible for the lack of change. It's my life, and I blame myself for the outcomes.

Even though I have people looking out for me, there are times when their support feels insufficient. In those moments, I become consumed by the darkness within me. I hesitate to make decisions simply because I want something desperately. I recognize that it may not be the right course of action at the present moment.

During my darkest times, I think negatively about myself. It's a challenging experience, having this moment of believing that I may never live up to the person I've dreamed of becoming and the version of myself I want the world to see. Although those moments come and go, I am self-aware. I understand that I can't dwell there because it can very easily become a jail.

Learning the Power of Freedom
We often desire freedom, but sometimes we struggle to understand how to use it wisely. Many believe that freedom means being able to do whatever we want, however we want,

as if there are no limits. But true freedom comes when we recognize our value and realize that we can move forward without being held back.

Freedom is a gift given to us when we no longer participate in the negativity that surrounds us. It is up to us to determine how we will utilize this freedom. We may have the freedom to choose, yet still find ourselves imprisoned by our own sins.

When I started following God, I discovered the power of freedom. It was in my hands to decide whether I would return to my old ways or use my freedom to pursue what is necessary for me to walk in purpose. Sometimes we forget just how precious freedom is, and we don't know how to handle it.

With freedom, we have the power to speak out, to make our voices heard, and to shape our own destinies. At times, we may find ourselves questioning if we truly have freedom or if we are still confined by the expectations of the world.

The freedom you seek is within your grasp, but you must understand that it is up to you to use it wisely. In my upbringing, I had freedom, but I felt trapped in a world that made me question my worth for a long time. I believed I had control, but in reality, it had control over me.

Freedom was available, and it was my responsibility to discern whether it was just a joke or a real opportunity for me to pursue and benefit from. Anything we hold inside ourselves that shouldn't be there acts as a prison, but we have the power to release those burdens.

Finding freedom is a personal journey. It requires accepting the truth and freeing ourselves from the things that hold us captive. However, we may not even realize that we are prisoners of what we carry within because our perspective is limited. We fail to see the bigger picture and forget that we have the power to change and claim the freedom we deserve. Fear often prevents us from embracing what is rightfully ours. We become so accustomed to staying within our comfort zones and not thinking outside the box that we forget there is a whole world outside waiting for us. We fail to consider whether the outside even exists, but beyond those limits lies our freedom, already present and waiting for us to take the first step.

When I finally tasted the air outside the proverbial box, I felt a big difference. I realized there was more to freedom, and I understood that I needed to actively seek it. At the same time, I recognized that I was on my own in this pursuit, responsible for seeking the things that being in the box had previously prevented me from experiencing.

There were moments when I questioned if freedom truly existed, moments when it seemed like just a word with no substance. But there is so much more to freedom than meets the eye. It is not merely a word; it holds great power.

Know that freedom is not just an abstract concept but an important part of your identity that the world may try to keep you from seeing or understanding. Once you embrace that part of yourself, nothing can hold you back because you understand your true value and potential.

When I found my freedom, the world became a different place for me. Even though I was sometimes insecure, I always believed that my happiness with freedom depended solely on me and how I chose to use it. I refused to live as if freedom didn't exist for me.

Freedom means being liberated from negative thoughts and toxic people. You have the power to free yourself from anything that holds you back and from the limitations that others impose upon you. You are free now, and it is up to you to pursue your dreams with the knowledge that you are no longer bound.

We all love receiving things for free, so why not free ourselves from the things that hold us back? Why not free ourselves so that we do not pay the price of being dishonest with ourselves? When I found my freedom, I broke free from every negative thought and every negative person around me. If I had the strength to persevere until I discovered what freedom truly meant and that I could extract that freedom from it, you have the power to do the same. It will completely transform your life.

CONCLUSION

The concept of villains is often associated with negative people who challenge us and make our journey more difficult. However, villains can also serve a purpose in our lives. They push us to fight harder and strive for our dreams. Even if we believe we have lived a clean life, we may unknowingly be the villain in someone else's story.

In my story, the villains were the ones who made me doubt myself and believe that I could never amount to anything. But their skepticism fueled my will to prove them wrong, not based on their judgment but on my own self-belief. Being a villain is often seen as a negative thing, with people talking about the harm they cause. However, they often push us to go further and become better versions of ourselves.

Sometimes the presence of the villain in your life can be overwhelming and even lead to thoughts of self-destruction. Take that moment as an opportunity to learn how to fight the battle and realize that you can overcome it. The villains may even haunt you in your dreams because you constantly think about them. It is a reflection of your own allowance for their presence, and if you can let them in, you can also kick them out. Before doing so, it's important to learn from their tactics and find ways to survive.

Even when things are going well, villains may continue to emerge and make you uncomfortable. There will always be a villain somewhere in the story, whether at the beginning or the end. They may trap you in situations where escape seems impossible, but learning how to manage and fight them will lead you to victory. You may lose some battles initially, but you will learn from your mistakes.

On the flip side, when we become the villain, we don't realize it. As humans, we tend to perceive ourselves as perfect and flaw-free, while easily recognizing the flaws in others. It's essential to reflect on our own actions and intentions to avoid becoming the villain in someone else's story.

Throughout my life, I have had many villains, particularly during my time at the orphanage. They played a significant role in shaping who I am today, even though they were unaware of their impact. They made me doubt myself, but ultimately helped me discover my true identity.

Villains, despite their negative aspects, contribute to the authenticity of our stories. Facing trials and persecution with a villain involved makes the narrative more realistic, almost like a real-life movie.

In my final days at the orphanage, it felt like I was living in a movie. It resembled the show "Once Upon a Time," where I was trying to get out of Storybrooke. The villains didn't want me to leave yet wanted to lead, requiring my assistance to fulfill their destiny. The villain possessed a good heart but lacked understanding of love, resulting in hurtful actions. It was only by showing her the power of love and the realization that ruling is not the key to everything that she began to change.

Ultimately, villains can be defeated with love. Don't give up on becoming a better version of yourself, knowing that villains cannot overpower you. You are the hero of your story, and while you may not choose who the villains are, you can choose whether you emerge victorious or succumb to the villain that has known you from the beginning.

Don't give up on trying, play your role effectively, and the villains will give up on trying to hinder your dreams. And remember, even if you strive to be the good guy, you may inadvertently become the villain in someone else's story due to our inherent human flaws and mistakes.

I've mastered the art of swallowing my emotions and pretending that everything is okay. While I can't claim to have endured the greatest suffering in life, throughout this book, you have seen that I have surely had my fair share of challenges. I've always prioritized others' happiness over my own, willing to bear the pain silently if it means someone else can have a good life.

The Little Orphan Who Hides Thousands of Feelings Behind

I hide my feelings so that others can freely express theirs, ensuring that they never know I am hurting. It's a selfless act, as I believe people shouldn't have to think about me when I appear to be doing well. Yet, deep inside, I am wounded. One thing that troubled me during my time at the orphanage was the lack of genuine care we received. If you choose to be a mother or father figure, you must act like one, rather than pretending to be one. Often, we make mistakes without realizing it. Maybe they didn't realize they were falling short.

I ended up burying my feelings because I knew no one would listen to my cries, even if I tried. With so many of us in the orphanage, there simply wasn't enough attention to go around. I once mustered the courage to bring this up to the president and some leaders, only to be met with the response that there were too many of us for them to give individual attention simultaneously. It made me think about pastors who care for large congregations. They manage to take care of their flock, providing support when they are hurt and someone to talk to.

I continued hiding my feelings, even when I had run out of space to store them. I bought more space within myself just to store the multitude of emotions I had felt and experiences I had gone through. The worst feeling in life is pretending to be someone you're not, pretending that everything is fine while deep down, you're crying every single minute. As an orphan, I believed my words were worthless, and expressing my feelings would only get me in trouble. I tucked my feelings behind my back, ensuring no one would notice my pain, while I pretended to be happy, yet shedding invisible tears.

Hiding your feelings is a form of self-deception. It may hurt to know the truth but continuing to lie to yourself can make everything seem real. Real life is acknowledging your pain and voicing it, not pretending to be okay while you're slowly withering away inside. One of my biggest mistakes was pretending to be happy when I wasn't. It was my fault that no one saw it because I never spoke up. We all hide our feelings, hoping someone will magically heal us, but it doesn't work that way. We need to show where we are hurting to find healing. We must speak up for ourselves.

I hid my feelings as if I were digging my own grave, aware that I would eventually find myself buried in them. Your feelings are valuable; don't go around pretending everything is fine when you're suffering inside. It takes years to heal from this, and it's not an easy journey. However, it is not impossible to find healing. I concealed my feelings as if nothing was wrong, as if life was perfect. I could be hurting at the orphanage, yet when groups visited, I would put on a happy facade, acting as if everything in my life was fantastic.

I couldn't heal because I continued pretending that I wasn't hurt. Know that your feelings can slowly destroy you. The cure to this is to stop pretending that you are fine.

Is "I'm Sorry" Enough?

I've learned to recognize that I apologize not because I could have done better, but because those actions were a part of me, and there was little I could do to prevent them at the time. Once it was over, I knew I was wrong, and I regretted my choices.

When I say, "I'm sorry," I don't just utter the words and continue making the same mistakes. Instead, I take a deep breath, learn from my mistakes, and move forward, leaving them behind me. Saying sorry means acknowledging what happened and striving to do better next time.

However, I must admit that I despise hearing that phrase from others. It bothers me when people knowingly do something hurtful and then come to me with a half-hearted apology. Once you've done something more than twice, it is no longer a mistake. It is a choice.

I try my best not to engage in behavior that requires an apology. I avoid that sentence as much as I can. I'd rather think twice, avoid hurtful actions, and if I do make a mistake, address it with a heartfelt note explaining my remorse, rather than casually saying "I'm sorry" without true consideration.

As I was growing up, I heard that phrase so often that I began to resent it. It became like a dish I ate repeatedly until I grew sick of it. There's nothing inherently wrong with apologizing, but when it becomes a password used to mend every heart you've broken with your thoughtless words, it loses its sincerity.

I often wonder, if someone breaks up with you over the same issue repeatedly, how many times would you go back to them? The same principle applies to saying sorry. Many of us fail to see that.

It hurts when you repeatedly make a child cry over the same matter, and eventually, that child starts to dislike what caused their tears. Sorry can bring relief, but it can also be a weapon that gradually kills the people around you.

Sometimes, sorry doesn't truly mean sorry. It becomes an expectation that everyone should say it, so why should I carry the weight of my guilt alone?

What I've learned is that in certain situations, saying sorry isn't enough. Sometimes, a warm hug or demonstrating that you never intended harm can have a bigger impact. Actions do speak louder than words, and saying sorry while continuing the same hurtful behavior is not a genuine solution.

Being The Exception

You are the exception, no matter what happens to you. You are unique and set apart. When you have faith, it sets you apart from the rest. Just because your parents went through something doesn't mean you have to go through the same experiences. Often, we mistakenly believe that because our parents or family members suffered, we are destined to follow the same path. But you are wrong. You are the exception. You are different and chosen by God to break free from the chains that have held your family down.

Don't feel compelled to be like your friends who may struggle with anxiety, depression, or loneliness. You are the exception. You are the one who will bring about change and transform everything around you and within you. Don't succumb to the negative patterns of your family. It's your time to shine brighter than ever and make the exception.

Remember, every rule has an exception. In the rule of your family dynamics, you are the exception, and that puts you in charge. You don't have to follow the same path as everyone else. You are not confined to the limited circle they have created. You are the exception.

I've come to realize that each and every one of us from the orphanage was the exception. We were chosen to be lights and to defy the definition of being an orphan. An orphan is not merely a child without parents; it is a child chosen by the Lord and a child who will redefine what it means to be an orphan.

If your family has experienced tragedy, such as suicide or depression, remember that you are not defined by their struggles. You are the exception. You have gone through a lot because you are meant to be the exception. However, that doesn't mean you have to continue being stuck in that cycle. Show them that you are the exception and that nothing can stop you.

For a long time, you may have observed how your family was always there for everyone but themselves, and you may have thought you had to be the same way. But now it's time to recognize that you are the one who will make the exception. From today onwards, you are free from the rules. You don't have to follow them because you are the exception.

If you feel scared or uncertain about being the exception, remember why you were called and that you were chosen. Your name stands out, and now you have the opportunity to make a difference. Believe that you can do it, even if it takes time to fully embrace your exceptional nature. Don't forget your identity and heritage. You are the exception, and though it may take time to truly feel it, I assure you that you are.

It took me 18 years to realize that I was an exception, right from the moment I was born. So if you don't feel like you are the exception yet, take your time. When the right moment comes, you will see yourself as the exception. Embrace your uniqueness, for being the exception makes you truly special.

Never give up because you are not alone. Have confidence in knowing that the One who initiated a good work in you will carry it to completion until the day of Christ Jesus (Philippians 1:6). Don't abandon your pursuits because God is with you. He didn't take you this far just to leave you stranded, but to guide you to where you belong.

It can be challenging to persevere when obstacles arise in your life. When faced with these obstacles, you may feel like giving up and believe that God has started something and left you to finish it on your own. But that is not the case. It's about not giving up, even when it feels like He is distant.

For as long as I can remember, I have never given up on the things I start. I may get annoyed and discouraged, but I always ask God to give me strength to persist. Even when I doubt and question why I started in the first place, deep down, I know He is present and will act at the right moment. If I had given up, I would never have reached where I am today.

Giving up is like working for an entire year and quitting just before receiving your annual payment. It means losing everything you've earned and everything that could make your life easier and better. Don't give up just because the process takes time or because you feel like it's not worth it. You cannot start something and stop halfway through, pretending it wasn't worthwhile. You must keep going and not give up.

In this life, strive to be good at everything except giving up.

When you refuse to excel at giving up, you will achieve what you never thought possible. My life is a mystery, and I love it because I believe that anything can happen. I believe that if I don't give up, I will obtain what I am seeking. I never give up because I know what awaits me at the end.

Do not give up because God will not abandon what He started. He will continue to work and fulfill His plans. Giving up is not the solution; if you quit, you lose, and I don't think you want to lose. Show others that you can persevere, even when it hurts. Life may not guarantee you anything, but it will teach you how to navigate it.

When you are pursuing your goals, remember that you are not alone, and you will never be alone. We often think that we are fighting battles or suffering alone, but that is not true. You are not fighting alone; you have someone beside you who is stronger than you are. And if you find yourself in a favorable position right now, don't think that you achieved it all by yourself. God was there to comfort you every time you wanted to give up and didn't have enough strength to continue. He was the one who sustained you throughout the journey, helping you overcome any obstacles in your path to reach your goals.

Now it's time for you to acknowledge that you were never alone in your endeavors. Even if you feel isolated in the process, He is right there with you. Don't give up because you are not alone.

Do you realize that even inside your mother's womb, God was there? Do you understand how many didn't make it or how many passed away shortly after birth? It serves as a powerful example to remind you that if you have arrived where you are, it is because you are not alone, and you will never have to face it alone.

It Was All A Puzzle

Life is like a puzzle, and each of us holds the pieces to our own unique picture. It's a complex puzzle that only we can put together for ourselves, with others playing their own unique role in our lives. Sometimes it takes hours, or even a lifetime, to understand the intricacies of our puzzle. Before the puzzle was broken into many pieces, it was a beautiful picture. It had to be cut into smaller pieces to make it a puzzle. After it has been put back together, it becomes this beautiful picture again.

At times, I found myself figuratively holding the puzzle box upside down, unable to see how the pieces fit together. It was only when I realized I was holding it upside down and turned it the correct way that I saw how huge my puzzle was. Working on it took more time than I thought, as I searched for the right pieces to connect.

Our lives are an ongoing puzzle that we can never truly finish because new pieces are added every day. It's important to recognize that our stories are puzzles too. If we don't acknowledge this, we may struggle to navigate through them. Each piece may look similar, but they all have their unique place and purpose in our puzzle.

I came to understand that there are different people who play a part in my story, and I am the one who holds everything together, like the box. The stories within me can only come out if I allow them to. Each piece belongs inside the box, but they cannot find their place until I figure out where they belong in the puzzle.

Some pieces of my puzzle got chewed up or thrown away by people who didn't understand their value. They didn't know that if one piece is missing the picture will not be complete. Only later in life did I realize that those missing pieces were guilt, hate, selfishness, and other negative aspects. To find those missing pieces and repair the chewed-up ones, I needed to discover my true identity in Christ. He alone can mend the broken pieces and restore them to their original state.

Our lives are like puzzles, and they can be challenging or straightforward, depending on the choices we make and how we arrange our pieces. I remember a time when my mother and I attempted a difficult puzzle. Many pieces looked alike, and the picture itself was ugly. I didn't have the strength to continue because the picture did not inspire me.

Similarly, our own life puzzles can be messy and filled with difficulties. We may feel like giving up, not realizing that the finished puzzle can be beautiful. It's easy to walk away from a puzzle because it's hard, but the true joy lies in staying committed and completing it. It's a testament to our perseverance and hard work.

Remember, you are not alone in putting your puzzle together. Don't give up, for you will find great people who can help you along the way. Together, we can conquer the challenges and create a beautiful picture from the pieces of our lives.

NEVER ALONE

GUIDED JOURNAL

This journal is designed to be your compassionate companion on a journey of self-discovery, healing, and growth. Abandonment and loneliness are profound experiences that can leave lasting imprints on our hearts and minds. They may arise from various life circumstances such as loss, rejection, or a sense of disconnection from others. While these feelings can be overwhelming, it's important to recognize that you are not alone in your struggle. This journal is here to remind you that healing is possible and that you have the inner strength to navigate this journey with courage and resilience.

Within the pages of this journal, you will find a series of affirmations accompanied by a bible verse, curated to guide you through the process of healing and reframing your mind concerning abandonment and loneliness. As you embark on this journaling venture, it's essential to remember that healing is a nonlinear process. Some days may be more challenging than others, and that's okay. The intention of this journal is not to provide quick fixes or instant solutions, but rather to create a safe space where you can explore your feelings and experiences at your own pace.

Remember, healing is a courageous act of self-love. By embarking on this journaling journey, you are taking an important step towards reclaiming your power, finding solace, and transformation.

May this journal serve as a comforting and transformative tool as you navigate the depths of your emotions and emerge stronger, wiser, and more connected to yourself and the world around you.

With love and support,

Carmenta Jean Baptiste

I was created to be strong and courageous.

_____

Deuteronomy 31:6 - "Be strong and courageous. Do not be afraid or terrified because of them, for the LORD your God goes with you; he will never leave you nor forsake you."

The Lord receives and accepts me, even when others may forsake me.

Psalm 27:10 - "Though my father and mother forsake me, the LORD will receive me."

I have no reason to fear or be discouraged because God strengthens and helps me.

_____

_____

_____

_____

_____

_____

_____

_____

_____

_____

_____

_____

_____

_____

_____

_____

_____

_____

_____

_____

_____

_____

Isaiah 41:10 - "So do not fear, for I am with you; do not be dismayed, for I am your God. I will strengthen you and help you; I will uphold you with my righteous right hand."

In my brokenness, the Lord is near, comforting and saving me.

_____

_____

_____

_____

_____

_____

_____

_____

_____

_____

_____

_____

_____

_____

_____

_____

_____

_____

_____

_____

Psalm 34:17-18 - "The righteous cry out, and the LORD hears them; he delivers them from all their troubles. The LORD is close to the brokenhearted and saves those who are crushed in spirit."

There is no place I can go where God's presence cannot reach me.

_____
_____
_____
_____
_____
_____
_____
_____
_____
_____
_____
_____
_____
_____
_____
_____
_____
_____
_____
_____
_____
_____

Psalm 139:7-8 - "Where can I go from your Spirit? Where can I flee
from your presence? If I go up to the heavens, you are there; if I
make my bed in the depths, you are there."

I can be strong and courageous because the Lord
goes with me wherever I go.

_____

_____

_____

_____

_____

_____

_____

_____

_____

_____

_____

_____

_____

_____

_____

_____

_____

_____

_____

_____

_____

_____

_____

Joshua 1:9 - "Have I not commanded you? Be strong and
courageous. Do not be afraid; do not be discouraged, for the LORD
your God will be with you wherever you go."

The promise of God's eternal presence brings me comfort and reassurance.

_____
_____
_____
_____
_____
_____
_____
_____
_____
_____
_____
_____
_____
_____
_____
_____
_____
_____
_____
_____
_____
_____
_____

Matthew 28:20 - "And surely I am with you always, to the very end of the age."

God will never leave or forsake me, regardless of my circumstances.

_____

_____

_____

_____

_____

_____

_____

_____

_____

_____

_____

_____

_____

_____

_____

_____

_____

_____

_____

_____

_____

_____

_____

Hebrews 13:5-6 - "Keep your lives free from the love of money and be content with what you have, because God has said, 'Never will I leave you; never will I forsake you.' So we say with confidence, 'The Lord is my helper; I will not be afraid. What can mere mortals do to me?'"

As I seek God, He will never abandon me but will always be faithful.

Psalm 9:10 – "Those who know your name trust in you, for you, LORD, have never forsaken those who seek you."

I am redeemed and called by name; I belong to the Lord.

_____

_____

_____

_____

_____

_____

_____

_____

_____

_____

_____

_____

_____

_____

_____

_____

_____

_____

_____

_____

_____

_____

Isaiah 43:1 - "But now, this is what the LORD says— he who created you, Jacob, he who formed you, Israel: 'Do not fear, for I have redeemed you; I have summoned you by name; you are mine.'"

God sets the lonely in families and brings joy to those who feel imprisoned.

_____
_____
_____
_____
_____
_____
_____
_____
_____
_____
_____
_____
_____
_____
_____
_____
_____
_____
_____
_____
_____
_____
_____
_____
_____
_____

Psalm 68:5-6 - "A father to the fatherless, a defender of widows, is God in his holy dwelling. God sets the lonely in families, he leads out the prisoners with singing; but the rebellious live in a sun-scorched land."

I may face difficulties and persecution, but I am not abandoned or destroyed.

---

2 Corinthians 4:9 - "persecuted, but not abandoned; struck down, but not destroyed."

God heals my broken heart and binds up my wounds.

Psalm 147:3 - "He heals the brokenhearted and binds up their
wounds."

The Lord's love and care for me surpasses any human love; I am always remembered by Him.

Isaiah 49:15-16 - "Can a mother forget the baby at her breast and have no compassion on the child she has borne? Though she may forget, I will not forget you! See, I have engraved you on the palms of my hands; your walls are ever before me."

14

I am not an orphan, for God comes to me and dwells within me.

_____

_____

_____

_____

_____

_____

_____

_____

_____

_____

_____

_____

_____

_____

_____

_____

_____

_____

_____

_____

_____

_____

John 14:18 – "I will not leave you as orphans; I will come to you."

Nothing can separate me from the love of God that is in Christ Jesus.

Romans 8:38-39 - "For I am convinced that neither death nor life, neither angels nor demons, neither the present nor the future, nor any powers, neither height nor depth, nor anything else in all creation, will be able to separate us from the love of God that is in Christ Jesus our Lord."

I can pour out my troubles to the Lord, knowing that He is my refuge.

_____

_____

_____

_____

_____

_____

_____

_____

_____

_____

_____

_____

_____

_____

_____

_____

_____

_____

_____

_____

Psalm 25:16-17 - "Turn to me and be gracious to me, for I am lonely and afflicted. Relieve the troubles of my heart and free me from my anguish."

God's love and compassion for me are unshakable, even in times of upheaval.

_____
_____
_____
_____
_____
_____
_____
_____
_____
_____
_____
_____
_____
_____
_____
_____
_____
_____
_____
_____

Psalm 68:6 - "God sets the lonely in families, he leads out the prisoners with singing; but the rebellious live in a sun-scorched land."

In the darkest valleys, I have no reason to fear, for the Lord is with me.

_____

_____

_____

_____

_____

_____

_____

_____

_____

_____

_____

_____

_____

_____

_____

_____

_____

_____

_____

_____

_____

_____

_____

_____

Isaiah 54:10 - "Though the mountains be shaken and the hills be removed, yet my unfailing love for you will not be shaken nor my covenant of peace be removed," says the LORD, who has compassion on you.

Even in abandonment by others, the Lord stands by my side and strengthens me.

_____
_____
_____
_____
_____
_____
_____
_____
_____
_____
_____
_____
_____
_____
_____
_____
_____
_____
_____
_____
_____

Psalm 23:4 - "Even though I walk through the darkest valley, I will fear no evil, for you are with me; your rod and your staff, they comfort me."

God has anointed me to bring good news and freedom to the brokenhearted and captives.

----

2 Timothy 4:16-17 - "At my first defense, no one came to my support, but everyone deserted me. May it not be held against them. But the Lord stood at my side and gave me strength, so that through me the message might be fully proclaimed and all the Gentiles might hear it. And I was delivered from the lion's mouth."

From the Sovereign Lord comes deliverance from death and darkness.

Isaiah 61:1 - "The Spirit of the Sovereign LORD is on me because the LORD has anointed me to proclaim good news to the poor. He has sent me to bind up the brokenhearted, to proclaim freedom for the captives and release from darkness for the prisoners." 22

In times of loneliness and neglect, I find refuge and portion in God alone.

Psalm 68:20 - "Our God is a God who saves; from the Sovereign LORD comes escape from death."

When I pass through trials and challenges, God is with me, protecting and guiding me.

Psalm 142:4-5 - "Look and see, there is no one at my right hand; no one is concerned for me. I have no refuge; no one cares for my life. I cry to you, LORD; I say, 'You are my refuge, my portion in the land of the living.'"

I am rescued and protected by the Lord because I love and trust in Him.

_____
_____
_____
_____
_____
_____
_____
_____
_____
_____
_____
_____
_____
_____
_____
_____
_____
_____
_____
_____
_____
_____

Isaiah 43:2 - "When you pass through the waters, I will be with you; and when you pass through the rivers, they will not sweep over you. When you walk through the fire, you will not be burned; the flames will not set you ablaze."

In every circumstance, I can trust God as my refuge and source of strength.

_____
_____
_____
_____
_____
_____
_____
_____
_____
_____
_____
_____
_____
_____
_____
_____
_____
_____
_____
_____

Psalm 91:14 - "Because he loves me," says the LORD, "I will rescue him; I will protect him, for he acknowledges my name."

I acknowledge that the Lord is my portion and will wait upon Him.

Psalm 62:8 - "Trust in him at all times, you people; pour out your hearts to him, for God is our refuge."

I cast all my worries and anxieties on God, knowing that He cares for me.

_____

_____

_____

_____

_____

_____

_____

_____

_____

_____

_____

_____

_____

_____

_____

_____

_____

_____

_____

_____

_____

Lamentations 3:24 – "I say to myself, 'The LORD is my portion; therefore I will wait for him.'"

Trusting in God at all times, I find solace and safety in His embrace.

---

1 Peter 5:7 - "Cast all your anxiety on him because he cares for you."

I need not fear, for God is with me, gathering and bringing me close to Him.

_____

Isaiah 43:5 - "Do not be afraid, for I am with you; I will bring your children from the east and gather you from the west."

ABOUT THE AUTHOR

Carmenta Jean Baptiste was an orphan who defied the odds. Born and raised in Haiti, Carmenta faced a challenging childhood marked by uncertainty and a lack of familial connection as a result of being placed in an orphanage at the tender age of four.

Her life took a remarkable turn when she discovered the power of faith. Through her  unwavering belief in God, she transformed from a young girl raised without love to a woman overflowing with compassion for others.

Carmenta's journey led her to the United States. and serves as a testament to the transformative power of faith, perseverance, and self-belief. She now navigates her path as an inspirational figure, motivated by a personal mantra, "From orphan to Oprah" to become the fullness of who she was created to be.

Carmenta understands that not all readers share her Christian faith, but she firmly believes that regardless of one's beliefs, there is a plan for your life. She encourages individuals to embrace their worth and recognize that they are more than enough, deserving of all life has to offer.